Experiencing War

This edited collection explores aspects of contemporary war that affect average people – physically, emotionally, and ethically – through activities ranging from combat to drawing war.

The aim of this work is to supplement the usual emphasis on strategic and national issues of war in the interest of beginning to theorize war from the point of view of individual experience, be the individual a combatant, a casualty, a supporter, opponent, recorder, veteran, distant viewer, an international lawyer, an ethicist or an artist. This volume presents essays that push the boundaries of war studies and war thinking, without promoting one kind of theory or methodology for studying war as experiential politics, but with an eye to exploring the possibilities and encouraging others to take up the new agenda. It includes new and challenging thinking on humanitarianism and war, new wars in the Third World, gender and war thinking, and the sense of the body within war that inspired recent UN resolutions. It also gives examples that can change our understanding of who is located where, doing what with respect to war: women warriors in Sierra Leone, war survivors living with their memories, and even an artist drawing something seemingly intangible about war – the arms trade.

The unique aspect of this book is its purposive pulling together of foci and theoretical and methodological perspectives from a number of disciplines on a variety of contemporary wars. Arguably, war is an activity that engages the attention, the politics, and the lives of many people. To theorize it with those lives and perspectives in mind, recognizing the political contexts of war, is long overdue.

This inter-disciplinary book will be of much interest to students of war studies, critical security studies, gender studies, sociology, and IR in general.

Christine Sylvester is Professor of International Relations and Development at Lancaster University, UK, and the recent recipient of the annual Kerstin Hesselgren Chair in Sweden.

Series: War, Politics and Experience
Series editor: Christine Sylvester

Experiencing War
Edited by Christine Sylvester

Experiencing War

Edited by Christine Sylvester

Routledge
Taylor & Francis Group

LONDON AND NEW YORK

First published 2011
by Routledge
2 Park Square, Milton Park, Abingdon, Oxon OX14 4RN

Simultaneously published in the USA and Canada
by Routledge
270 Madison Avenue, New York, NY 10016

*Routledge is an imprint of the Taylor & Francis Group,
an informa business*

The right of the editor to be identified as the author of the editorial
material, and of the authors for their individual chapters, has been asserted
in accordance with sections 77 and 78 of the Copyright, Designs and
Patents Act 1988.

Typeset in Times by
GreenGate Publishing, Tonbridge, Kent
Printed and bound in Great Britain by
TJ International Ltd, Padstow, Cornwall

British Library Cataloguing in Publication Data
A catalogue record for this book is available from the British Library

Library of Congress Cataloging-in-Publication Data
Experiencing war / edited by Christine Sylvester.
p. cm.
1. War – Psychological aspects. 2. War and society. I. Sylvester, Christine.
U22.3.E858 2010
303.6'6—dc22
2010018474

ISBN: 978–0–415–56630–8 (hbk)
ISBN: 978–0–415–56631–5 (pbk)
ISBN: 978–0–203–83999–7 (ebk)

To Swati, Sungju, Lyn, and Cami

Contents

Contributors

Stephen Chan is Professor of International Relations, and former Dean of Law and International Relations at the School of Oriental and African Studies (SOAS), University of London. He is the author of numerous articles and several notable books, including *Out of Evil: New International Politics and Old Doctrines of War* (2005), *Robert Mugabe: A Life of Power and Violence* (2003), and most recently, *The End of Certainty: Towards a New Internationalism* (2010). He is also a published poet and a martial arts master.

Jill Gibbon was born in Australia and moved to the UK in 1979. An artist, activist and art historian, she reverses the usual focus of war art on the war zone by drawing the military-industrial complex. She has a BA in graphic design from Leeds Polytechnic, an MA in art history from Keele University, and a PhD in reportage drawing from Wimbledon School of Art/University of Surrey. She teaches Arts and Humanities at the Open University.

Brigitte M. Holzner is Director of Gender and Development for the Austrian Ministry of Development. Before that, she was a lecturer in the Women, Gender, Development program at the Institute of Social Studies, The Hague, and a researcher on Indonesia and post-socialist countries. She has written most recently on 'Legal Pluralism in the Family Law: Implications for Development Policy' (2009), and 'Agrarian Restructuring and Gender – Designing Family Farms in Central and Eastern Europe' (2008).

Kimberly Hutchings is Professor and Head of the Department of International Relations at the London School of Economics. She works on a range of areas within the field of international political theory, including feminist ethics, critical IR theory, and the relation between politics and violence. Her recent books include *Time and World Politics: Thinking the Present* (2008) and *Global Ethics: An Introduction* (2010).

Heonik Kwon is a Reader in Anthropology at the London School of Economics. He is the author of several articles and the books *The Decomposition of the Cold War* (2010), and *Ghosts of War in Vietnam* (2008), which won the Kahin Prize of the Association for Asian Studies. He is interested in cold war culture, death rituals and the politics of memory, kinship in political history and theory, and the role of creative cultural practice in conflict resolution.

Megan MacKenzie is a lecturer in Political Science and International Relations at the University of Victoria, New Zealand. Prior to joining the department, she was doctoral fellow at the Belfer Center for International Security and the Women and Public Policy Program at the Kennedy School, Harvard University. She is the author of 'Securitization and De-securitization: Female Soldiers and the Construction of the Family', *Security Studies* (2009) and 'Empowerment Boom or Bust? Assessing Women's Post-Conflict Empowerment Initiatives', *Cambridge Review of International Affairs* (2009), and has a related book in progress for New York University Press.

Anne Orford is the inaugural holder of the Michael D. Kirby Chair of International Law and an Australian Research Council Professorial Fellow at Melbourne Law School, where she is also the foundation Director of the Institute for International Law and the Humanities. Among her books are *Reading Humanitarian Intervention: Human Rights and the Use of Force in International Law* (2003), the forthcoming *International Authority and the Responsibility to Protect*, and the forthcoming *Cosmopolitanism and the Future of International Law*.

Christine Sylvester is Professor of International Relations and Development at Lancaster University, UK, and Kerstin Hesselgren Chair, Sweden, 2010–11. She has authored two books on international relations, including *Feminist International Relations: An Unfinished Journey* (2004), two on Zimbabwe, including *Producing Women and Progress in Zimbabwe* (2000), and the recent *Art/Museums: International Relations Where We Least Expect It* (2009). She has also edited *Critical Works in Feminist International Relations* (2010), a five-volume compendium, and has a book series with Routledge: War, Politics and Experience.

Acknowledgements

This volume features the work of a few of the many speakers that contributed to the Touching War programme I organized and directed at Lancaster University over a seven-month period in 2008–2009. I would like to thank the funders of that project: the Institute of Advanced Studies at Lancaster University, the Department of Politics and International Relations at Lancaster, and the Lancaster University Film Society. I wholeheartedly thank all the contributors to this volume and all of the following, most of whom participated in Touching War:

April Biccum
Bruce Bennett
Israel Butler
Helen Caton
Patricia Chilton
Feargal Cochrane
Rachel Cooper
Gerry Davies
Bulent Diken
Mervyn Frost
Lola Frost
Jennifer Glasse
Paul Gough
Patrick Hagopian
Mary Hamilton
Andrew Humphreys
Athina Karatzogianni
Adi Kuntsman
Mark Lacy
Vicky Mason
Cristina Masters
Chris May
Amalendu Misra
Kyoko Murakami

Jude Murison
Shuruq Naguib
Pat Noxolo
Malachi O'Doherty
Swati Parashar
Gale Parchoma
Sungju Park-Kang
Corinna Peniston-Bird
Elina Penttinen
Mike Roper
Cami Rowe
Peter Rowe
Laura Sjoberg
Dan Smith
Graham Smith
Annabelle Sreberny
Jayne Steel
James Summers
Denny Taylor
Lyn Warrener
Michael Weil
Anita Wilson
Joseba Zulaika

1 Experiencing war

An introduction

Christine Sylvester

War is a repetitive politics of violence that crosses human history. No one is immune from its touch: there are pieces of war in peacetime and pieces of peace in war. Sadly, the practices of violent politics show few signs of letting up, giving up, or relinquishing a hold on the imaginary of international politics and over the lives of so many people caught up by it. This collection takes the last phrase of that sentence as its starting point: the lives of so many people. It draws our attention away from strategic and national interest politics of war to the prospect of theorizing war from a starting point in individuals, the ones who experience war in the myriad ways possible – as combatants, casualties, voyeurs, opponents, artists, healers, grave diggers, and so many other identities. What unites them all is the human body, a sensing physical entity that can touch war, and an emotional and thinking body that is touched by it in innumerable ways. But there are also many divides – cultural, religious, historical, national, generational, linguistic, gender, race, class that can lead to conflict. Difference exaggerated, invented, or politicized in the extreme can explode into large-scale armed conflict between groups that find others so "other" that they must be killed. Weapons and bodies then get aimed at other bodies, even if they are said to be aimed primarily at "strategic targets," "pockets of resistance," armed opponents and the like. A key characteristic of war in practice is that it engages and acts on bodies.

Judith Butler knows this. She advocates an approach to theorizing war, and to building a politics to stop it, that pays consummate attention to wartime emotions common to friend and enemy alike: mourning, grieving, feeling inexplicable loss. She asks:

> What form political reflection and deliberation ought to take if we take injurability and aggression as two points of departure for political life ... [knowing] that there are others out there on whom my life depends, people I do not know and may never know.[1]

Historians who talk to warriors and veterans also know that bodies are the locus of powerful war experiences. Christian Appy hears a former Lieutenant General in the US Marine Corps struggle with his lingering Vietnam War emotions:

Trainor once wrote that the Vietnam War produced a "genie of anguish" that he had bottled up inside. Asked to elaborate he says, "Well, I still can't go to the Vietnam Veterans Memorial." With these words he suddenly chokes up. A dam of emotion seems about to break, but within seconds he regains control ... "Deep down there's a hurt and I don't know what it is. I can't control it. It's always there and I think I'll just live with it for the rest of my life."[2]

The famous British war photojournalist, Don McCullin, writes books and exhibits his pictures from all the wars he saw through the lenses of cameras and felt through the skin on his body and pulsations in his brain. Writing of his time with the Biafran secessionist forces in 1969, McCullin offers a telling aside about taking food

> and other things for the children of a man called Chinua Achebe, one of the genuine idealists on the Biafran side. He was a novelist, who wrote a book called *Things Fall Apart*. That was precisely what was happening now. He was a young man, an honourable man, a nice man. I remember the last time I saw him. He took the gifts without any emotion. He had cut off any feeling he may once have had for the one or two Westerners he thought really cared. I felt he was looking through me as if I didn't really exist. And I could see that the ruin of the Ibo culture had made him feel exactly as I had when coming out of Hue [Vietnam] – totally shell-shocked.[3]

Not all bodies in war experience the "genie of anguish" – at least not all the time. A former soldier on the Vietnamese side admits that the war was very often a depressing experience. But he also says:

> How could you allow yourself to be depressed when you saw people making their homes inside the hulk of a tank like this? [He points to one of his photographs of a Vietnamese family living inside the remains of a destroyed U.S. tank.] Looking at people like them, we knew our task wasn't finished. They were the real source of our psychological motivation.[4]

Miranda Allison interviewed a woman in the Irish Republican Army of Northern Ireland who told her that joining up "was not a personal experience and it was not emotional. ... No, I thought very long and hard and I thought how best to achieve what I believed in, and I believed that that was the way forward."[5] Some people embrace war, get addicted to it, celebrate it, and keep lining up for it by displaying horrendous weapons at arms fairs or by becoming iteratively mercenary. They might live comfortably in the Green Zone of Baghdad or feed off it, willingly or most likely not, like Mother Courage did during the Thirty Years War, and like the kidnapped bush women had to do during the Liberian civil wars.[6] Or they can isolate themselves from threats around them and thereby make the situation of their otherness very obvious: "The American military closed off streets near its bases in the city, regardless of whether they were vital thoroughfares ... The sight of barricaded roads was a daily reminder to Iraqis that they were under occupation."[7]

This collection has its origins in a program of events I planned and directed at Lancaster University over the 2008–9 academic year. It was called Touching War.[8] For seven months, a variety of speakers, round tables, discussion groups, workshops, films, and studio art sessions probed war as a bodily set of experiences. The program was inspired by the realization that global communications leave few people in today's world isolated from and unaffected by specific wars or the constancy of war ethics, war economies, war language, and or actual combat around them. Rather than focus, as many do in the field of international relations, on military strategy, battlefield tactics, weaponry, foreign policy, or causes and correlates of war, Touching War considered many ways that people in different locations touch war and are touched by it in physical, emotional, and intellectual ways. Those physically and emotionally proximate to war have different experiences to those at more distance from it. Fiction writers and artists experience war through the characters they invent or the marks they make. Scholars who research war have different reference points for war experiences to those who engage in war for a living. No one's narrated experience or research, therefore, can be considered final and complete. We all touch war or are touched by it nonetheless.

War itself, though, is a difficult phenomenon to pinpoint beyond the now inadequate sense that it always involves armed conflict between states. In the post-World-War-II era, armed conflict can envelop states and entities other than states. Wars that do involve states are rarely declared or conducted in the pitched battles of yore that ended with one side decisively winning. Anti-colonial wars, cold war proxy wars, genocidal or separatist wars, communal wars, humanitarian interventionist wars, and wars against terror characterize the post-war period. These can remain unfinished, as they are in parts of the Middle East, flaring up episodically and morphing in form over years. They can be highly asymmetrical, with professional soldiers facing hit-and-run militias or hidden resistant communities. Wars are conducted today using high-tech weaponry flung from the air, robotic machines, computers, and also machetes wielded by neighbors. War-fighting strategies encompass rape and individual suicide plus other forms of physical assault that directly challenge established international law (on humane treatment of prisoners, for example). Touching War confronted the varieties of armed conflicts that have helped define the second half of the twentieth century up to today with bodily experience in mind.

To theorize war from the multi-pointed view of experience is long overdue. This collection, therefore, pushes the boundaries of critical and conventional war studies and war thinking. It does not promote one kind of theory, definition, approach, or methodology but rather explores new possibilities of conceptualizing aspects of an old social institution and its practices. In doing so it draws on perspectives from law, history, art history, anthropology, ethics and philosophy, development studies, international relations, and art practice. Focusing specifically on post-cold-war wars, it offers challenging thinking on humanitarianism and war, on so-called new wars in Africa, on cold war memories, the women's bodies of war that inspire recent UN resolutions, and war as a repeating exception to laws against killing, a repeating cycle of technological innovation and arms trade, and a repeating anointment of war artists to sketch the next war. It lays out arguments for focusing more on the politics of war as human experience than is usually the case in the social sciences, particularly in war studies and political science, and brings readers war-relevant literatures that they might not be familiar with in strict disciplinary contexts.

The undertaking begins with a chapter that is fittingly by the first speaker in the Touching War program: law professor Anne Orford, who traveled to Touching War from Melbourne University. "The passions of protection: sovereign authority and humanitarian war" addresses this question: does the existence of vulnerable bodies in wartime, especially those experiencing pain, serve as a break on the militarized power of states or does it in fact urge on state authority and power? She asks that question in the context of humanitarian interventionist warring, a form of post-cold-war intervention that Orford previously criticized the legal profession for defending;[9] it is a form of warfare that I describe as "kill some to be kind to others."[10] Humanitarian intervention is carried out by major military powers in situations where there can seem to be no other way to protect the lives of suffering people caught up elsewhere in civil wars, insurgencies, or failed state scenarios. It is interventionist war backed up by the legal concept of sovereign responsibility to protect. Orford shows how major states can be both opposed to cruelty in war and willing to impose cruelty on civilian populations through a form of warring meant to protect them, or more accurately protect their theoretical freedoms. Orford's discussion of contradictions in humanitarian intervention and law is compelling, not least because it confronts the continuing tendency to reaffirm the state as the rightful subject of war – and the United Nations acting universally in its name – not individual people affected by state violence. Appealing to ideas from widely varying times and locations, including political philosophy, art, and poetry, Orford launches the book by asking readers to rethink responsibility, protection, and authority as they relate to bodies that are touched violently by war, yet are placed, in effect, off stage by international law.

The next chapter takes the discussion of experiencing war in a related direction by considering the ethics of gender and humanitarian war. Kimberly Hutchings, Professor of International Relations at the London School of Economics, focuses on moral rather than legal issues in "Gendered humanitarianism: reconsidering the ethics of war." She argues that humanitarian intervention actually operates not by universalizing the human to be rescued from suffering, but by reproducing assumed gender differences between people. Some bodies are deemed rescuers and others (women and children) are nearly always cast as needing rescue and protection from villains by heroes. Some feminist work in international relations would circumvent gender-based dichotomies by distinguishing between kinds of violence and by building feminist theory of war making around certain kinds and circumstances of violence only. Hutchings does not see this as a solution to the gender differentiation problem. Needed is greater contemplation of moral authority and moral agency when addressing the relational ethics of humanitarianism, not a recalibration of degrees of gender responsibility, authority, deservedness, and agency. For her, a violent moral agency based on gendered fictions of any kind would not be the way forward.

These early chapters, each addressing issues of bodies and ethics surrounding humanitarian intervention, are followed by two pieces that bring specific bodies of war to light: women in the wars of Bosnia-Herzegovina, Liberia, and Sierra Leone. Brigitte M. Holzner, Head of the Gender and Development Department of the Austrian Government, and a former colleague at the Institute of Social Studies, The Hague, has considerable experience working with bodies of war in the global south. In "Wars, bodies, and development" she writes about gender-based violence in the Bosnian and Liberian wars as the backdrop or prelude to UN actions to recognize gender-particular challenges in war zones. UN resolutions 1325 and 1888 endeavor, in effect, to render women more human, more rights-bearing, before wars, in wars, and in post-conflict deliberations. The resolutions endeavor to bring experiences that have been habitually subsumed in the term "civilian" into clear view and thereby into the politics of war and recovery. In effect, the UN authorizes a new inclusion to the sovereign-like passion for protecting "passive" women in wartime, namely, an emphasis on women's participation in wars and in peace. However, Holzner's own observations in the field indicate that the UN has not nuanced the identity "women" in ways that escape the usual dichotomous associations with victimhood and war prey. A propos of Hutching's concerns, at issue for Holzner is how to deal with the reinstatement of old gender ideas in war by institutions that are mandated to reject war or pacify it.

Megan MacKenzie, a lecturer in politics at Victoria University of Wellington, New Zealand, offers a glimpse of women as soldiers in Sierra Leone and compares the stories they tell about their experiences in war with the myths of war that keep reinstating "women soldiers" as always already exceptions to the standard male soldier. Like Holzner, MacKenzie argues that international organizations like the UN have simplified or standardized women's and girls' activities in war. They assume that brutalities associated with that war, the amputations and mass sexual violence that were part of war in Sierra Leone, were instigated and carried out by men. When women admit to fomenting or participating in such cruelties of war, they are treated as so exceptional as women as to be entirely mad. Drawing on personal interviews she conducted in situ, MacKenzie starts to separate the myths from the realities, the rule from the many rules of engagement in a war such as Sierra Leone's. Given the horrors discussed, it is little wonder that international organizations, academics, and the media simplify, dichotomize, and try to fix women's experiences as less brutalizing than men's. Still, the truth behind the stories that MacKenzie reports cannot be domesticated.

Heonik Kwon, a Reader in Anthropology at the London School of Economics, is an expert on wars of the cold war era and the memory experiences they have left behind. His "Experiencing the cold war" telescopes the fifty years of conflict that existed in international relations between World War II and the era of new wars of the twenty-first century. The cold war is described in the West in terms of bitter ideological enmity between the US-led alliance of "free" states and the socialist states under the authority of the Soviet Union. That "war" was new for the Western countries in the sense that all-out nuclear war was always within sight and clearly prepared by the key alliance actors. Yet some have termed the cold war era the long peace, because the USA and the USSR did not go to war with one another. Hot wars in other parts of the world served as proxies for direct alliance confrontation. Kwon helps us experience the cold war through small communal moments that feature family memorabilia or ancestral tales told about people involved in (cold war) local wars. The people Kwon talks about are geospatially distant from each other, but their struggles with memory and forgiveness are similar, whether they occur in post-war Greece, or in Vietnam, Indonesia, or Korea. The point Kwon makes is for families touched by war, any narrative of the cold war that focuses only on state-to-state threats in Europe or North America misses something important: the power hierarchies of that era that make it possible for even losers of cold war wars, like the USA in Vietnam, to write the history of the era of Vietnam in their own ways. Lost is a sense of everyday life in places where cold war wars actually raged, and lost as well are important continuities between those wars then and how they can affect people now.

We then come to Stephen Chan's contribution on the nature of what have been called new wars of our post-cold-war time. New wars is a term that ostensibly describes the wars, conflicts, atrocities, and combatants that Holzner and MacKenzie are seeking to understand. But Chan, who has considerable experience in Africa as an academic, diplomat, and government consultant, is not having this new wars tag. New wars are said to exist outside all strictures of the Geneva Convention by virtue of their unfathomable irrationality of cause and wanton means of installing regional and world order chaos amidst heaps of maimed or slaughtered bodies. From his perch as Professor of International Relations at the School of Oriental and African Studies, University of London, Chan argues that the modus operandi of these wars is not necessarily new. In some cases, the approaches are recycled as generation after generation takes up where their forebears left off (Afghanistan). In other cases, the grievances of the moment may be trumped up or exaggerated; but the weapons and technologies used to organize the wars are conventionally modern, even if they are operationalized from within caves or while on the run. What is new is the spectacle made out of the bodies of war and the combinations of old and new that horrify so much that researchers find it difficult to shift their eyes from the perpetrators to the experiences of war that survivors can narrate.

The final contribution runs strongly with an idea of art and war that resonates with art mentioned in earlier pieces, but not in ways many readers might anticipate. Jill Gibbon is a British anti-war activist and trained artist and scholar. I am most grateful to Gerry Davies of the Lancaster University Art Department for arranging her visit to campus for Touching War. Jill draws, among other things, the arms trade that sustains militarism and war. That is not an easy thing to do. It entails attending arms trade shows and surreptitiously drawing what she sees of people experiencing weapons close up, buying them, drinking to them, flirting with them and their purveyors, fondling little weapon-toy souvenirs. She writes about the experience of clandestinely entering the shows and then working quickly to interpret and draw the social scenes she sees there. She proceeds with an eye on linking her unconventional effort to a long tradition of war artists working within war zones. The war artist witnesses a war via images and can be inspired to artistic greatness by it. Jill's agenda is more complex. The results of her observations take the viewer to a commercial facet of war making, war thinking, war loving, war sexing, and war bodies. One of her drawings features on the cover of this book.

In the final chapter, I consider the collection as a whole and some theoretical and methodological directions that future research on war as experience could take. The focus is on legal/ethical/organizational concerns, shifting locations of war experience, and ordinary people's tales of war as a realm of memory, gender relations, and emotion.

Notes

1 Judith Butler, *Precarious Life: The Powers of Mourning and Violence* (London: Verso, 2004), p. xii.
2 Bernard Trainor, quoted by Christian Appy, *Vietnam: The Definitive Oral History Told From All Sides* (New York: Ebury Press, 2003), p. 8.
3 Don McCullin, *Unreasonable Behaviour: An Autobiography* (London: Vintage, 2002), p. 122. Chinua Achebe's classic novel *Things Fall Apart* (New York: Fawcett, 1959) brilliantly renders an Ibo society disrupted to the point of tragedy by the seemingly innocent and then increasingly challenging presence of early Christian missionaries, who settled in an area that would be part of Biafra.
4 Duong Thanh Phong, quoted in Appy, *Vietnam*, p. 249.
5 Quoted in Miranda Allison, *Women and Political Violence: Female Combatants in Ethno-National Conflict* (London: Routledge, 2009), p. 146.
6 Bertolt Brecht, *Mother Courage and Her Children*, Tony Kushner, trans. (London: Methuen, 2009); Danai Gurira, *Eclipse* (not published), a play performed at the Yale Repertory Theater, New Haven Connecticut, October 2009.
7 Rajiv Chandrasekaran, *Imperial Life in the Emerald City: Inside Baghdad's Green Zone* (London: Bloomsbury, 2007), p. 262.
8 See the entire program at http://www.lancs.ac.uk/fass/events/touchingwar/. Touching War was funded by the Institute of Advanced Studies, the Lancaster University Film Society, and the Department of Politics and International Relations at Lancaster University.
9 Anne Orford, *Reading Humanitarian Intervention: Human Rights and the Use of Force in International Law* (Cambridge: Cambridge University Press, 2003).
10 Christine Sylvester, "The Art of War/The War Question in (Feminist) IR," *Millennium: Journal of International Studies* 33, 3, 2005, p. 870.

2 The passions of protection

Sovereign authority and humanitarian war

Anne Orford

Late in 2007, I attended a workshop that brought together senior legal military advisers – from NATO, the UK, the US, Ireland, the Netherlands, Fiji, Sri Lanka and Sweden – with NGO representatives and academics, in order to discuss the relevance of gender to international humanitarian law. International humanitarian law is the body of international law that governs the conduct of parties to armed conflict. I felt a little anxious when the first proposal for institutionalizing gender neutrality to emerge from the workshop involved ensuring that female as well as male figures should pop up as targets during shooting practice. At the end of our two days together, one of the formerly sceptical senior military lawyers told the group that he was a convert to gender analysis. 'Gender issues aren't just personnel issues', he announced enthusiastically. 'They are intelligence issues! Gender is a force multiplier – if you understand how gender works in a particular society, you can control that society much more effectively!' Perhaps, in what Rey Chow has called 'the age of the world target', this should not have surprised me.[1] Chow argues that since at least the dropping of the atomic bombs on Nagasaki and Hiroshima, to become an object of knowledge is to become a potential target. So to introduce gender, or bodies, or human suffering, into the system for producing knowledge about war automatically means that knowledge about gender, or bodies, or human suffering, becomes part of the targeting machine.

In this chapter, I would like to explore the relationship between the vulnerability of human bodies and the logics of state power and militarism. Do suffering bodies accuse or resist power by their very presence? Or might the recollection of human vulnerability and the representation of suffering in fact reinforce or justify power? After all, vulnerable bodies – bodies in pain – are everywhere in representations of war today. Activist websites focused on the situation in Darfur, such as the 'Passion of the present' site or that of the 'Save Darfur' campaign, combine the language of salvation with images of suffering to mobilize military action in the name of our common humanity. The photographs and descriptions of the infliction of pain upon detainees in the camps at Abu Ghraib and Guantanamo have caused outrage around the world. The many recent books about those whom Philippe Sands has named the 'torture team' describe in excruciating detail the violence inflicted upon the bodies of those interrogated in the detention centres and prisons controlled by the US and its allies.[2] Yet somehow, the two sets of images or scenes of suffering remain separate. The centrality of the US military to much humanitarian strategizing has not been seriously challenged. While much of the human rights movement has been properly appalled by the abuses carried out by US military and security forces in the war on terror, advocates of humanitarian intervention still do not question whether increased intervention by the US military under its current rules of engagement offers the best strategy for the protection of individuals in Darfur or elsewhere. Indeed, in many critical appraisals of the conduct of the war on terror, politicians and their advisers are indicted, while the US military and the laws of war are redeemed. According to legal scholars such as Philippe Sands and Scott Horton, the torture of detainees represents an abandonment of the disavowal of cruelty in warfare by the professional US military.[3] Sands, for example, describes the interrogation practices involved in the war on terror as a departure from US military tradition, a tradition in which 'the US military did not "do" cruelty or torture'.[4] Sands traces this tradition back to the general orders promulgated by President Lincoln in 1863, stating: 'Military necessity does not admit of cruelty'.[5]

At the same time, the push for greater military intervention in the name of protecting suffering peoples in Africa, Asia and the Middle East has received an enormous boost through the adoption of the notion of the 'responsibility to protect' in international relations. The language of the responsibility to protect has gradually colonized the legal and political debate internationally since its development by the International Commission on Intervention and State Sovereignty or ICISS in 2001.[6] ICISS was an initiative, sponsored by the Canadian government, which was designed to respond to the perceived tension between state sovereignty and humanitarian intervention in the aftermath of the NATO action in Kosovo. When the 'responsibility to protect' concept was introduced into the mainstream institutional debate by the ICISS report, it was presented as a new way of talking about humanitarian intervention, as well as a new way of talking about sovereignty. Both were organized around protection. The new way of talking about sovereignty was to argue that 'its essence should now be seen not as control but as responsibility'.[7] If a state is unwilling or unable to meet this responsibility to protect its population, it then falls upon the international community to do so. The new way of talking about humanitarian intervention involved re-characterizing the debate 'not as an argument about any right at all but rather about a responsibility – one to protect people at grave risk'.[8] The people at grave risk were those '[m]illions of human beings' who, in the words of the ICISS report, 'remain at the mercy of civil wars, insurgencies, state repression and state collapse'.[9]

Institutionally, the 'responsibility to protect' concept has been successful in a way that humanitarian intervention never was. A range of actors, from US counter-insurgency specialists, through UN officials to human rights activists and Christian aid workers, have enthusiastically begun to redescribe and reconceptualize their missions in terms of protection. These actors have also begun to integrate activities across a remarkable range of areas within a protection framework. UN agencies from the Office of the UN High Commissioner for Refugees to the World Health Organization now work in protection clusters when they are in the field. At the UN, two senior positions have been created to implement the responsibility to protect – Edward Luck was appointed to the new position of Special Adviser to the Secretary General on the Responsibility to Protect in 2008, and Francis Deng was appointed to the newly styled position of UN Special Adviser on the Prevention of Genocide in 2007. UN Member States have also embraced the concept, apparently with much greater willingness than was the case with humanitarian intervention. Member States voted unanimously in the General Assembly at the 2005 World Summit to adopt the responsibility to protect as an obligation both of individual Member States and of the international community,[10] and since then representatives of states including the UK, the US, France, Sweden and Australia have specifically invoked the responsibility to protect to explain actions taken or proposed by their governments.

I am interested in this chapter in making sense of the relation between these two features of contemporary international humanitarianism – the claim that the modern military state, and in particular the US, has abandoned cruelty as an official instrument of warfare, and the claim that it is through increased international policing and military intervention that the state can be perfected and protection of those at risk achieved. First, I begin to explore this relation by looking at the way in which international humanitarian law incorporates the killing or wounding of civilians within the calculations of military statecraft. Then I turn back to the early history of the modern state to try to make sense of the ways in which international humanitarian law and military practice sanctify certain kinds of killing or wounding in the name of preserving the security of the commonwealth. Finally, I conclude by asking what this relationship between law, violence and the modern state means for understanding, and responding to, the logics of humanitarian warfare.

The calculation of suffering

Both international humanitarian law and the broader legal prohibition against torture during war or peace can be understood as part of a modern project to eliminate what international law describes as 'cruel, inhuman or degrading treatment or punishment'.[11] Humanitarian intervention can be understood as an extension of that project – as an attempt not just to prohibit but to eliminate certain forms of suffering in this world. Central to this task is the distinction between torture and cruel, inhuman or degrading treatment on the one hand, and justifiable suffering on the other. The infliction of pain is accepted in many modern states as part of 'warfare, sport, scientific experimentation, and the death penalty',[12] and more controversially as part of sexual and artistic practice. Military historians have written 'of the new practices of "deliberate cruelty"' employed in war over the twentieth century, from the use of mines filled with jagged metal fragments designed to tear and fracture bodies, to napalm with its ingredient that 'increases the adherence of the burning petrol of human skin surfaces' through to possession of chemical, biological and nuclear weapons of mass destruction that advertise 'governmental readiness to inflict cruel death'.[13] Yet while war 'is the most obvious analogue to torture',[14] it remains the case that the normal and lawful conduct of war is not understood to involve 'cruel, inhuman or degrading treatment or punishment'. Torture and cruelty thus refer to suffering that is essentially gratuitous from the perspective of the state. International law, like modern statecraft, envisages that certain kinds of suffering are authorized. Some forms of suffering are understood as necessary or inevitable – in particular, the suffering that is authorized in terms of the reason of state or proportional to military necessity. That which is prohibited is suffering that is excessive, suffering that is beyond that calculated as necessary to protect state security or to enable human flourishing. It is on the basis of this logic that the use of military force against peoples and territories in Africa, Asia and the Middle East can be understood as humanitarian, or that aerial bombardment can be understood as humane.

We can see this logic in action if we look at the ways in which international humanitarian law deals with the killing and wounding of civilians. The norms of international humanitarian law prohibit the targeting of civilians in armed conflict, requiring attackers to direct their actions against broadly defined 'military objectives' rather than 'civilian objects'.[15] Civilians can be killed 'incidentally', but the risk of endangering civilians through 'collateral damage' must not be disproportionate to the military advantage to be gained by the attack.[16] The utilitarian language of this balancing test reveals that the lives of civilians can be sacrificed if the value of their existence is weighed against the importance of 'military objectives' and found wanting. Similarly, while it is illegal to target purely civilian infrastructure, 'dual use' infrastructure can be targeted. 'Dual use' relates to infrastructure that serves both a civilian and a military function. For instance, roads, electricity distribution systems and communications networks might all have this dual function depending on the extent to which they form part of the 'command and control' aspect of a state's military activities. Of course, attacks on such 'targets' can also have severe effects on the lives of civilians. The 'harm to the civilian population' caused by attacks on dual use targets must therefore be weighed against the military objectives that such attacks are calculated to achieve.[17]

As this brief description reveals, international humanitarian law immerses its addressees in a world of military calculations. As General Michael Rose sums this up, 'the aim of the law of war is to save life and limb by encouraging humane treatment and by preventing *unnecessary* suffering and destruction'.[18] International humanitarian law addresses us as if we were all military strategists, for to determine when suffering and destruction is 'necessary' requires adopting a strategic perspective. In this sense, international humanitarian law reinforces the aesthetic effect of modern televised forms of warfare, in which the audience is invited to occupy the position of the soldier or strategist. 'Sighting the target' involves converting 'the object into information as a condition of the violence directed towards it'.[19] The viewer of such images participates both 'in the sighting and eliminating of the enemy target', and does so in a situation in which there is not even 'the mediated sense of presence and context experienced by the soldiers viewing the same image in their cockpits and tanks'.[20]

The extent to which civilian deaths are seen as legitimate in conflict situations is dependent also upon the determination of the facts of each case. In a subtle way, this also involves taking the perspective of the state in many situations of modern warfare. In international law, as in domestic law, the application of law depends upon the determination of 'facts'. In the case of international humanitarian law and its capacity to protect civilians, these 'facts' include decisions about whether the targeting of a particular object to further a military objective may pose a risk to civilians, and whether particular infrastructure is 'dual use'. Determination of these facts itself depends upon the information provided by intelligence services. This becomes increasingly complicated in times of 'network-centric' warfare such as that conducted in Iraq in 2003, where coalition forces relied upon US intelligence and surveillance systems on the battlefield.

The implications of this for the utility of international humanitarian law are illustrated by institutional responses to the criticism of the conduct of the NATO bombing campaign, Operation Allied Force, carried out against the Federal Republic of Yugoslavia from 24 March to 10 June 1999. During that 78-day campaign, NATO dropped more than 25,000 bombs, killing an estimated 500 Yugoslav civilians. These deaths resulted partly from the use of cluster bombs, attacks on targets in densely populated urban areas, attacks on mobile targets, use of depleted uranium projectiles and the practice of dropping bombs from extremely high altitudes to avoid pilot deaths.[21] Attempts to bring the issue of whether this conduct violated international humanitarian law before international judicial fora were remarkably unsuccessful.[22] The Office of the Prosecutor (OTP) at the International Criminal Tribunal for the former Yugoslavia (ICTY) received 'numerous requests that she investigate allegations that senior political and military figures from NATO countries committed serious violations of international humanitarian law' during the bombing campaign.[23] However, in June 2000, the Chief Prosecutor announced to the Security Council her decision not to initiate an investigation of the claims that NATO had engaged in serious violations of international humanitarian law in the former Yugoslavia, based upon the report of a committee she had established to investigate the matter.[24] Of particular interest here are the ways in which that committee had treated the information and intelligence gathered by NATO in its evaluation of the legality of target selection. In explaining its recommendations, the committee stated:

> One of the principles underlying international humanitarian law is the principle of distinction, which obligates commanders to distinguish between military objectives and civilian persons or objects. The practical application of this principle is effectively encapsulated in Article 57 of Additional Protocol I [to the Geneva Conventions] which, in part, obligates those who plan or decide upon an attack to 'do everything feasible to verify that the objectives to be attacked are neither civilians nor civilian objects'. The obligation to do everything feasible is high but not absolute. A military commander must set up an effective intelligence gathering system to collect and evaluate information concerning potential targets. The commander must also direct his forces to use available technical means to properly identify targets during operations. Both the commander and the aircrew actually engaged in

operations must have some range of discretion to determine which available resources shall be used and how they shall be used.[25]

According to the committee, international humanitarian law thus requires states to 'set up an effective intelligence gathering system to collect and evaluate information concerning potential targets'. Having set up such a system, the military then has 'some range of discretion' in evaluating that 'information concerning potential targets'. The committee was then strongly influenced both by NATO's perception of the legitimacy of its targets and the information NATO had gathered to form that perception. While NATO's targets included 'some loosely defined categories such as military-industrial infrastructure and government ministries and some potential problem categories such as media and refineries', it was the committee's view 'that NATO was attempting to attack objects it perceived to be legitimate military objectives'. The committee found that NATO forces did attack, *inter alia*, a civilian passenger train (killing at least 10 civilians), a convoy of refugees (killing approximately 70 to 75 civilians), the Serbian television and radio station (killing between 10 and 17 civilians), the Chinese Embassy (killing three civilians) and Korisa village (killing as many as 87 civilians, mainly refugees). Overall, 495 civilians were killed and 820 civilians wounded in documented instances. However, based upon explanations provided by NATO officials, NATO's military analysis and the impression they gained by viewing cockpit videos from NATO planes, the committee members concluded that civilians were not *deliberately* targeted in these incidents and that legitimate mistakes were made by NATO in the conduct of its campaign. In addition, the committee concluded that while there was evidence that NATO forces had dropped depleted uranium and cluster bombs during their campaign, these weapons – though they make it very difficult to distinguish between civilians and combatants – were not absolutely prohibited in all situations and their use in this case should not be further investigated.[26]

The prior question to 'who applies the law?' must always be 'who determines the facts?' and 'who determines which facts are relevant?' Facts cannot simply be found. In domestic legal systems, the removal of ambiguity through the writing of facts and the determination of their relevance is part of the practice of judgment.[27] In the world of military strategy that informs the reasoning of international humanitarian law, a great deal of deference is paid to the intelligence, and therefore the sovereign authority, of powerful states. Thus while some protection is offered to civilians by international humanitarian law, this protection is offered within a framework in which strategic calculations about military necessity and state survival are privileged, and in which facts are often determined by the intelligence of the attacking state. Having adopted this perspective, it becomes difficult to argue with the targeting expert who asserts that striking a particular target is proportional and necessary. The deaths of civilians, the ruination of cities, the destruction of livelihoods and the pollution of the environment can ultimately be justified if these means are deemed proportional to the ends of military necessity.

Indeed, this was the conclusion that the International Court of Justice (ICJ) reached in a remarkable opinion in which the question of the legality of the killing of civilians and the primacy of state security was directly addressed – the 1996 Advisory Opinion on the *Legality of the Threat or Use of Nuclear Weapons*.[28] On 15 December 1994, the General Assembly adopted a resolution requesting the ICJ urgently to render an advisory opinion on the question: 'Is the threat or use of nuclear weapons permitted under international law?'[29] In its Advisory Opinion, the Court confirmed that international humanitarian law applied to nuclear weapons. This flowed from the

> intrinsically humanitarian character of the legal principles in question ... which permeates the entire law of armed conflict and applies to all forms of warfare and to all kinds of weapons, those of the past, those of the present and those of the future.[30]

The Court noted that the first cardinal principle contained in the texts of international humanitarian law is

> aimed at the protection of the civilian population and civilian objects and establishes the distinction between combatants and non-combatants; States must never make civilians the object of attack and must consequently never use weapons that are incapable of distinguishing between civilian and military targets.[31]

The Court recognized the unique characteristics of nuclear weapons, including the inability to distinguish between civilian objects and military objectives in the use of those weapons, the largely uncontrollable and necessarily indiscriminate effects of their use, and the enormous number of casualties that would result from the use of such weapons.[32]

Yet while the Court held that due to these characteristics, 'the use of such weapons in fact seems scarcely reconcilable' with the principles of international humanitarian law, it could not 'lose sight of the fundamental right of every State to survival, and thus its right to resort to self-defence ... when its survival is at stake'.[33] The Court thus held, by seven votes to seven, with the President providing the casting vote, that:

> while the threat or use of nuclear weapons would generally be contrary to the rules of international law applicable in armed conflict ... in view of the current state of international law, and of the elements of fact at its disposal, the Court cannot conclude definitively whether the threat or use of nuclear weapons would be lawful or unlawful in an extreme circumstance of self-defence, in which the very survival of a State would be at stake.[34]

This then is the logical if troubling conclusion to a form of law that treats the state as its principal referent. While international lawyers may at times see themselves as the representatives of a civilized conscience or shared sensibility that transcends the state, they still rely upon the state as the vehicle through which this universal law is to find expression. The international order brought into being through international law depends upon state power. States are the authors of international law, whether as negotiators of treaties or as generators of customary practice. States are the agents of coercion, whether through collective security mechanisms or resorting to force in self-defence or as countermeasures. States are the creators of courts and the implementers of international obligations domestically. Thus international law can have nothing to say in the face of the demand made by the modern state that, in some circumstances, the state must remain free to kill and maim those who threaten its existence.

Underpinning the legal recognition of the modern state as the *de facto* authority in the international system is the question of why this fact has a normative value. That question is no longer addressed in most accounts of the validity of international law. It is as if positive international law, like other forms of modern law, can no longer give an account of its own authority or even 'articulate the terms of its own existence'.[35] It is to that question of the grounds of the authority of the modern state and modern law that I want now to turn.

Protection, shock and awe

So far, this chapter has explored the implications of the representation of military statecraft as a rational process involving the weighing and balancing of individual life and state survival. I'd like now to argue that the history of the modern state suggests grounds for questioning even this claim that reasoned calculation governs the practice of statecraft. And while the rational explanation for state violence would seem to make human beings disposable, the irrational or perhaps passionate explanation for state authority renders us even more vulnerable.

The state is often represented as the ultimate achievement or expression of rationality. Modern state theorists certainly promoted the idea that obedience to the state was a rational choice on the part of its subjects. Thomas Hobbes, for example, famously urged moderns to understand that the commonwealth represented the individual's best chance for self-preservation in a time of civil war. In his classic treatise *Leviathan*, Hobbes sought to develop a theory that would explain why it was rational to submit to an absolute political authority capable of containing the warring religious factions threatening the continued existence of the commonwealth.[36] He did so at a time in which the legitimacy of public authority had become a serious question. The wars of religion that had been waged throughout Europe had undermined appeals to a universal and shared set of values that might ground political and legal authority.[37] Appeals to the truth of competing religious beliefs and the post-sceptical spirit of the new sciences were everywhere shaking the foundations of established political orders. In *Leviathan*, Hobbes therefore did not seek to ground authority upon inheritance, or conformity with custom or precedent, or upon a shared set of moral values or some authentic relationship with the people. For Hobbes, the authority of the state or the commonwealth was based upon its capacity to guarantee protection. Hobbes argued that an earthly power was needed to bring into being a condition in which the laws of nature could be realized on earth. In particular, the existence of a common power or common wealth would make possible the realization of the first and most fundamental of these natural or divine laws – that men '*seek peace and follow it*' – so that the right of each man to self-preservation could be guaranteed.[38] Men covenanted with each other as equals to bring into being such a commonwealth. Through that act of covenanting, the commonwealth was entrusted with sovereign power for a particular end, 'the procuration of *the safety of the people*'.[39] Individuals, according to Hobbes, should therefore harness their passion for self-preservation to the reason of the state.[40]

Something similar is being staged with the turn to protection as the basis of international authority today. The 'responsibility to protect' concept is presented as a rational solution to the problem of creating political order in situations where such order is non-existent or under threat. It is premised on the notion that authority, to be legitimate, must be effective. To quote former Secretary General Kofi Annan, 'the primary raison d'être and duty' of every state is to protect its population.[41] If a state proves unable to protect its citizens, the responsibility to do so shifts to the international community. The advocates of the responsibility to protect seek to make an argument for the lawfulness of both state and international authority, without reference to self-determination, popular sovereignty or to other romantic or nationalist bases for determining who should have the power to govern in a particular territory. Rather, the legitimacy of authority is determinable by reference to the *fact* of protection. This grounding of authority on the capacity to preserve life and protect populations rejects the more familiar claims to authority grounded on right, whether that right be understood in historical, universal or democratic terms. By focusing upon *de facto* authority, the 'responsibility to protect' concept implicitly asserts not only that an international community exists, but that its authority to govern is, at least in situations of civil war and repression, superior to that of the state. Yet for the advocates of the 'responsibility to protect' concept, as for Hobbes, this championing of a new form of authority is not understood to be a denial of freedom. Rather, freedom is only believed to be realizable under the protection of an authority with the capacity to safeguard the well-being of the population. What matters for those advocating the responsibility to protect is the effectiveness of the techniques available to achieve protection and the maintenance of a functioning security machine. War or police action may be necessary – and thus individual lives may have to be sacrificed – in order to protect a population at risk. The population here functions as a 'transcendental form of life' in the name of which mere 'biological life' can reasonably be sacrificed.[42]

Yet in the seventeenth century, and again today, reason cannot fully explain the violence unleashed by the state – or the international community – in the name of protection. Again, I think Hobbes helps to show why. Hobbes argued that for the commonwealth as the protective authority to last, more was needed than an appeal to reason. For Hobbes, 'there be somewhat else required (besides covenant)'.[43] In order for sovereignty to be 'constant and lasting', the common power must also act to keep the people in 'awe' (or perhaps 'shock and awe').[44] A 'visible power to keep them in awe' was necessary to ensure the performance of the covenants that found the commonwealth. Covenants might be binding, but 'covenants, without the sword, are but words'.[45] Fear and violence therefore have a complicated position in the theory of Hobbes. On the one hand, fear is the rational basis for submission to the Leviathan. Fear is a response to what Hobbes portrays as objective threats, such as the need to defend against attacks by other subjects or the violence of an invading power. On the other hand, fear is potentially as 'artificial' as the sovereign, in that the sovereign must perform as that visible power which keeps the people in awe if their agreement (and thus the commonwealth which it generates) is to last. Thus while Hobbes sought to persuade his readers that sovereign power is not the result of 'sacral authority' but rather comes about 'as a consequence of the rational acts of will of the people', he nonetheless suggested that 'the sovereign should not be demystified altogether'.[46]

It is in this sense that the modern state is the inheritor of the religious foundations of European law and authority.[47] In early modern Europe, no state could have commanded the unquestioned obedience that states take for granted today.[48] That kind of obedience, to the extent that it was owed, was owed to God. By the eighteenth century, Europe had witnessed the shift of authority from God and his worldly representatives to the state. Thus Kant could argue in 1797 that we should act as if certain things were true if to do so would help to move us towards the civil state, and that one of the things we should treat as if true is that 'all authority comes from God'.[49] Kant was very clear that the citizen owed total obedience to authority in the form of the state. The supreme power was constituted in order to secure '*the rightful state*, especially against external enemies of the people'.[50] 'The aim is not, as it were, to make the people happy against its will, but only to ensure its continued existence as a commonwealth'.[51] It follows from this counter-revolutionary reasoning that 'all resistance against the supreme legislative power, all incitement of the subjects to violent expressions of discontent, all defiance which breaks out into rebellion, is the greatest and most punishable crime in a commonwealth, for it destroys its very foundations'.[52] There can 'be no rightful resistance on the part of the people', because 'a state of right becomes possible only through submission' to the 'universal general will'.[53] Not long afterwards, Hegel would assert that 'man must … venerate the state as a secular deity'.[54]

As the state became identified with the task of preserving the commonwealth and thus realizing the laws of nature in this world, the violence of the state was in turn sanctified. According to Hobbes:

> The office of the sovereign, (be it a monarch or an assembly,) consisteth in the end, for which he was trusted with the sovereign power, namely the procuration of *the safety of the people*, to which he is obliged by the law of nature.[55]

It was that sense of protection as 'procuration of *the safety of the people*' that would translate into the broader jurisprudence of security and policing in the late seventeenth and eighteenth centuries in Europe,[56] and into the representation of war as a political instrument for realizing the will of the people in the nineteenth century.[57] War and policing would come to be understood as means for realizing the safety of the people. While this was perhaps already of concern in the Europe of Kant and Hegel, by the twentieth century the violence of the modern state – with its concentration camps, its fire bombs, its napalm and its Hiroshimas – would come to exceed not only rational justification, but also rational comprehension.

Something similar is happening with the tendency to sanctify the violence inflicted by the representatives of the international community during humanitarian war. Much of the pro-humanitarian intervention literature has tended to treat the international community as the benevolent representative of humanitarian universalism, and argued that its authority to protect those at risk in exceptional situations should not be limited by law. This tendency is perhaps best illustrated by the decision of the European Court of Human Rights in the cases of *Behrami and Behrami v France* and *Saramati v France, Germany and Norway*.[58] The Grand Chamber of the Court there declared inadmissible two cases in which applicants sought to hold European states accountable for the acts of their military personnel participating in the 'international security force' or the international 'civil administration' created under the auspices of the UN in Kosovo. The applicants in the *Behrami and Behrami* case were Agim Behrami (applying both on behalf of himself and his deceased son Gadaf) and his son Bekir Behrami, both of whom lived in the municipality of Mitrovica, Kosovo. In March 2000, Mitrovica was in the sector of Kosovo for which a brigade led by France as part of the international security force (KFOR) in Kosovo was responsible. On 11 March 2000 a group of boys, including Gadaf and Bekir Behmari, came across a number of undetonated cluster bombs while playing in the hills. The bombs had been dropped as part of the NATO bombardment of the area in 1999, and KFOR knew of their presence on the site. The children began playing with the bombs, one of which detonated, killing Gadaf and seriously injuring Bekir. The applicants alleged that the death of Gadaf and injury of Bekir violated Article 2 (the right to life) of the European Convention on Human Rights, as they were caused by the failure of the French KFOR troops to mark or defuse the undetonated bombs. The applicant in the *Saramati* case was Ruzhdi Saramati, who complained that his detention by and under the orders of KFOR between 13 July 2001 and 26 January 2002 violated his right to liberty and security (Article 5) and his right to an effective remedy (Article 13), that his lack of access to a court violated his right to a fair trial (Article 6) and more broadly that France, Germany and Norway had failed to guarantee the Convention rights of individuals living in Kosovo (in violation of their obligation under Article 1 to secure to everyone within their jurisdiction the rights and freedoms defined in the Convention).

In dismissing these cases against states involved in the Kosovo intervention, the Court found that it was not competent to review the acts of respondent states carried out on behalf of the UN.[59] It held that operations established by Security Council resolutions, such as that conducted in Kosovo, are 'fundamental to the mission of the UN to secure international peace and security'.[60] To subject the actions carried out under UN authority to 'the scrutiny of the Court' would 'interfere with the fulfillment of the UN's key mission in this field including, as argued by certain parties, with the effective conduct of its operations'.[61] The actions undertaken by the Member States were 'directly attributable to the UN, an organization of universal jurisdiction fulfilling its imperative collective security objective'.[62] The court identified the UN, and the states and personnel acting under its authority, with the universal. The representatives of universalism should not be asked to take responsibility for the effects of their actions, whether that be the failure to remove unexploded cluster bombs dropped by NATO, resulting in the death and disfigurement of a number of children (the Behrami case), or the detention of an individual for 18 months without trial (the Saramati case). Those acting under the authority of the UN represent human rights and the rule of law merely by their presence. In the words of the Danish submission to the Court:

> States put personnel at the disposal of the UN in Kosovo to pursue the purposes and principles of the UN Charter. A finding of "no jurisdiction" would not leave the applicants in a human rights' vacuum ... given the steps being taken by those international presences to promote human rights' protection.[63]

In this vision, state officials controlled territory and detained individuals, not as invaders or occupiers, but as agents of a broader universalism that transcends any particular political order. This focus on that which transcends the imperfections of the present order is illustrated well by the response of Jürgen Habermas to the Kosovo intervention. Habermas endorsed NATO's action on the basis that it was understood by Continental European states as

> an 'anticipation' of an effective law of world citizenship – as a step along the path from classical international law to what Kant envisioned as the 'status of world citizen' which would afford legal protection to citizens against their own criminal regimes.[64]

The proper measurement of humanitarian action was in terms of the extent to which it represented a further step along that path to the coming cosmopolitan order. It becomes difficult to envisage the proper limits to the use of force in the name of goals such as saving humanity, eradicating evil or bringing into being a cosmopolitan order that would protect citizens against 'their own criminal regimes'. What sacrifice could be disproportionate to such ends?

Life and critique

What then should a critical engagement with military statecraft entail? Do we moderns need to seek a more perfect calibration, a more precise balancing of the costs and benefits involved in warfare? International humanitarian law is in part a call to do just that – to calculate, to evaluate risk and measure the suffering that is justified to defend the state. Should we try to respond to this call by entering more fully into the world of 'impossible calculations', of 'secret debts', of 'the charges on the suffering of others'?[65] Should we take part in the ongoing task of differentiating lives to be saved, lives to be risked and lives to be sacrificed?[66] Should we consider it 'moral progress that such a calculation is even possible' – that individual lives count enough that counting deaths seems necessary?[67] If so, the refusal of the ICJ to engage in the political task of weighing the costs and balances of warfare is to be condemned as an abdication of the office of the judge as representative of sovereign authority.

Or should we instead refuse the call to make the suffering inflicted by modern wars, including humanitarian wars, comprehensible? This was the position taken by Martti Koskenniemi in response to the Advisory Opinion of the ICJ in the *Nuclear Weapons* case. According to Koskenniemi, the 'silence' of the Court was 'a wholly appropriate response to the issues at stake'.[68] The Court's silence was to be welcomed as enabling the voice of justice to be heard. 'The Court felt both the law and its own authority to be insufficient for determining the status of the massive killing of the innocent.'[69]

In one sense the Court simply declared its *inability* to make this calculation: declaring that it could not 'conclude definitively whether the threat or use of nuclear weapons would be lawful or unlawful in an extreme circumstance of self-defence, in which the very survival of a State would be at stake'. The law, and indeed language itself, can seem inadequate to grasp the reality of nuclear weapons and the destruction that they represent. An American Brigadier General who witnessed the first atomic bomb test from a bunker at Alamogordo commented: 'Words are inadequate tools … It had to be witnessed to be realized'.[70] The figure of the civilian who is touched by war, killed or injured during armed conflict or nuclear attack, thus stands at the limits both of language and of modern law. As the international lawyer Hersch Lauterpacht once wrote, 'If international law is, in some ways, at the vanishing point of law, the law of war is, perhaps even more conspicuously, at the vanishing point of international law.'[71]

But we might take the Court to be making a stronger point – that we *should* not look to law or defer to authority to determine the meaning of such violence. To illustrate this last point, I'd like to turn to an incident that accompanied the appearance by US Secretary of State Colin Powell before the Security Council on 5 February 2003.[72] Powell's appearance before the Security Council was designed to explain why the US could not 'risk' leaving Saddam Hussein 'in possession of weapons of mass destruction'.[73] As Maureen Dowd reported in the *New York Times*, in anticipation of the post-presentation press conference the UN threw a blue cover over the tapestry reproduction of Picasso's *Guernica* on display at the entrance to the Security Council, and then placed the flags of the Security Council in front of that cover.[74] This double veiling served to hide Picasso's famous anti-war image from the television cameras and thus from the global audience which would also judge the adequacy of Powell's information.[75] Why did it become untenable at that moment for the representative of the US to stand before that backdrop and explain the reasons for bombing the territory and people of Iraq? Perhaps this was simply because, as Maureen Dowd commented, 'Mr Powell can't very well seduce the world into bombing Iraq surrounded on camera by shrieking and mutilated women, men, children, bulls and horses'.[76] But perhaps it was also because the reproduction of *Guernica* would have served as a reminder that the horror of war lies in its return to the scene that was there veiled.

Guernica makes visible the excessive nature of the violence that founds authority. At the moment of constitution of a legal order, that founding violence is neither legal nor illegal. The legitimacy of the law and of authority is established only once that violence has succeeded in creating a new order, and even then only provisionally. Thus while the legitimacy of the law is in a sense guaranteed by the state, this is always subject to being unsettled. This is perhaps evidenced most clearly in cases of revolution. If a rebellion against an existing government succeeds, the violence of the rebels takes on the legitimacy of the state it founded – if the rebellion fails in founding a new form of the state, the use of force will not receive official legitimation.[77] It is precisely such a potential 'founding or revolutionary moment', a moment 'before the law', [78] that *Guernica* portrays. The ambivalence about the meaning of such revolutionary violence for Spain was central to the reception of *Guernica* at its first public display at the Spanish Pavilion of the Paris World Fair of 1937. The 'terror bombing' earlier that year of the town of Guernica, after which the painting took its name, was itself part of the ongoing Spanish civil war. [79] The bombing of Guernica was an event the meaning of which was still open at the time of the World Fair. It could only be given a settled meaning as legal or illegal once the revolutionary violence had ended. *Guernica* is thus troubling in part because it freezes time at that moment when the violence that may yet found a new law is not yet 'buried, dissimulated, repressed'. [80] While *Guernica* circulates as a symbol of democracy and a critique of fascist violence, and while Picasso came down firmly on the side of the Republican government in the Civil War, the painting also retains a sense of the ambiguity inherent in the use of force. As John Berger comments, '[t]here are no enemies to accuse' in the painting. [81] For Berger, the protest 'is in what has happened to the bodies'. Thus *Guernica* stands as a reminder of this 'silence walled up in the violent structure of the founding act'. [82]

In addition, *Guernica* memorializes an event in the history of warfare that may mark the limit of modern law's capacity to authorize force and to bury the dead. The bombing of the Basque town of Guernica by German planes and pilots flying for General Franco was the first time that aerial bombardment had been carried out against civilians in Europe. A sense of the horrors of the new form of warfare is clear in the news reports of the event. [83] *Guernica* gives form to the idea of the apocalypse unleashed by such violence, through the haunting series of its suffering victims. [84] In so doing, it makes visible the possibility that the capacity of law or the state to secrete this violence in its foundation may be exceeded by the new capacity to cause unprecedented levels of destruction.

Finally, *Guernica* points to that which exceeds the law, of that which even the law guaranteed by the sovereign cannot contain. For many contemporary viewers of the painting, it was a reminder of mortality. The surrealist poet Michel Leiris saw in the painting a death notice and a farewell:

> In the black-and-white rectangle of ancient tragedy, Picasso sends us our
> death notice: everything we love is going to die, and that is why right now it
> is important that everything we love be summed up into something unforget-
> tably beautiful, like the shedding of so many tears of farewell. [85]

Guernica is a reminder that at the foundation of modern state law is the memory
of a violence that cannot in the end be authorized – as the poet José Bergamín
wrote of his response to the painting in Picasso's studio: 'This shockingly naked
thing haunts us with the disturbing question of its anxiety'. [86]

Each of these themes resonates with contemporary warfare, and made it impossible for the reproduction of *Guernica* to be displayed on 5 February 2003. The
US, through its Secretary of State, was attempting to perform as a legitimate sovereign before both the Security Council and the mass audience of the subsequent
televised news conference. This performance of sovereignty was designed to
guarantee not only the US as sovereign over the territory called the United States
of America, but also as the sovereign that guarantees the international law the US
sought to bring into being at that performance. This was a version of the law in
its own image, an international law that could authorize the violence that the US
was soon to bring to bear upon the territory and people of Iraq. The tapestry of
Guernica was a reminder of the effects of the excessive force that comes before
the law – and so it disappeared behind its veils.

Perhaps then, as the veiling of *Guernica* suggests, we might better maintain a
protest about 'what has happened to the bodies' by refusing to give the devasta-
tion of war a pattern that is comprehensible or a meaning that is familiar. This was
the argument that Koskenniemi was making when he endorsed the silence of the
ICJ in the *Nuclear Weapons* case. Koskenniemi argued that we should not look to
'technical rules' nor defer to 'professional authority' to determine 'the meaning of
the massive killing of the innocent'.[87] Rather, he argued, 'we need to be able to say
that we know that the killing of the innocent is wrong not because of what chains
of reasoning we can produce to support it, but because of who we are'.[88] On this
reading, it is better to *refuse* the invitation made by state militaries and international
law – to refuse, in other words, to become part of a system that weighs up things that
are presented as substitutional one for the other – these human lives, those wounded
bodies, that sovereign state. Perhaps, after all, we should welcome the inability of
humanitarian law ever successfully to bury the dead.

Conclusion

In contemporary discussions about war and terrorism, passion and reason are often
presented as opposites. Passion is the term used to describe the investment of religious militants in the beliefs that drive their resort to violence in defence of a faith
and a form of life. Reason in contrast is the term used to describe the calculations
of statesmen and professional military leaders in defence of national security or in
pursuit of military objectives. In this chapter, I have suggested that the reason of
military statecraft is itself the expression of a passionate attachment to a form of life.

As Hobbes showed so clearly, the passion for self-preservation can be translated into the reason of state through the constitution of a common power. Sovereign authority in this tradition is responsible both for preserving life and for protecting the population, both for defending the people against its enemies and for keeping the people in awe. We might understand these disparate tasks of authority in the terms suggested by Michel Foucault – as the power to take life and to make live. [89] Yet the desire to protect the commonwealth or community thus constituted can itself prove a threat, both to the survival of the community and to the life of its members. How then might the limits and the ends of protection best be conceived?

Questions about the proper limits and ends of protective authority are raised today by the conduct of the war on terror, the embrace of the responsibility to protect at the UN, the integration of development and security in the work of international and non-governmental institutions, and the practices of state-building and international administration. The projects of international humanitarianism are motivated by the desire to preserve life and overcome suffering (even at the cost of taking life and inflicting suffering). The doctrines of responsibility and of protection that accompany these projects explain that those exercising power, whether as representatives of states or of the international community, are in fact guaranteeing the freedom of those they control, manage, kill and wound. In light of those developments, and at a time when the conflict in Darfur can be described as 'the passion of the present', it seems useful to reconsider the theological foundations of the state-making project. [90] The jurisprudence of protection that emerged out of the seventeenth-century wars of religion may still have something to offer for thinking about the proper limits of worldly authority. As that jurisprudence suggests, the representation of power in terms of an office or responsibility to protect involves not only legitimizing new forms of authority, but also marking out the proper limits to the interests of such authorities in the lives (and deaths) of their subjects. It is those questions of the limits and ends of protective authority that international humanitarianism is yet to address.

Notes

1 Rey Chow, *The Age of the World Target: Self-Referentiality in War, Theory, and Comparative Work* (Durham and London: Duke University Press, 2006).
2 Philippe Sands, *Torture Team: Deception, Cruelty and the Compromise of Law* (London: Allen Lane, 2008).
3 *Ibid*; Scott Horton, 'Military Necessity, Torture, and the Criminality of Lawyers' in Wolfgang Kaleck, Michael Ratner, Tobias Singelnstein and Peter Weiss (eds), *International Prosecution of Human Rights Crimes* (Berlin Heidelberg: Springer, 2007) 169–83.
4 Philippe Sands, above note 2, 62.
5 *Ibid.*
6 International Commission on Intervention and Sovereignty (ICISS), *The Responsibility to Protect* (Ottawa: International Development Research Centre, 2001), available at http://www.iciss.ca/pdf/Commission-Report.pdf.
7 Gareth Evans, 'From Humanitarian Intervention to the Responsibility to Protect' (2006) 24 *Wisconsin International Law Journal* 703, 708.

8 *Ibid.*
9 ICISS, above note 6, 11.
10 2005 World Summit, 14–16 Sept 2005, *2005 World Summit Outcome*, 138–9, UN Doc. A/60/L.1 (20 Sept 2005).
11 Talal Asad, *Formations of the Secular: Christianity, Islam, Modernity* (Stanford: Stanford University Press, 2003) 100–3.
12 *Ibid*, 113.
13 *Ibid*, 116–17.
14 Elaine Scarry, *The Body in Pain: The Making and Unmaking of the World* (Oxford: Oxford University Press, 1985) 61.
15 See generally A P V Rogers, *Law on the Battlefield* (Manchester: Manchester University Press, 2nd edition, 2004).
16 See further W J Fenrick, 'Targeting and Proportionality during the NATO Bombing Campaign against Yugoslavia' (2001) 12 *European Journal of International Law* 489.
17 Human Rights Watch, *International Humanitarian Law Issues in a Potential War in Iraq*, Human Rights Watch Briefing Paper, 20 February 2003, available at http://www.hrw.org/backgrounder/arms/iraq0202003.htm#5.
18 General Sir Michael Rose, 'Foreword to the first edition', in A P V Rogers, above note 15, xiv.
19 Michael P Clark, 'The Work of War after the Age of Mechanical Reproduction' in Michael Bibby, *The Vietnam War and Postmodernity* (Amherst: University of Massachusetts Press, 2000) 17, 28.
20 *Ibid.*
21 Human Rights Watch, *Civilian Deaths in the NATO Air Campaign* (2000).
22 See further Anne Orford, *Reading Humanitarian Intervention: Human Rights and the Use of Force in International Law* (Cambridge: Cambridge University Press, 2003) 192–4.
23 Final Report to the Prosecutor by the Committee Established to Review the NATO Bombing Campaign Against the Federal Republic of Yugoslavia, para 1, available at http://www.icty.org/x/file/About/OTP/otp_report_nato_bombing_en.pdf.
24 *Ibid*, 91 (recommendation by the Committee 'that no investigation be commenced by the OTP in relation to the NATO bombing campaign or incidents occurring during the campaign').
25 *Ibid*, 29.
26 *Ibid*, 26 and 27.
27 Nina Philadelphoff-Puren and Peter Rush, 'Fatal (F)laws: Law, Literature and Writing' (2003) 14 *Law and Critique* 191, 201.
28 *Legality of the Threat and Use of Nuclear Weapons*, Advisory Opinion, ICJ Reports, 1996, 26.
29 *Ibid*, 1.
30 *Ibid*, 85 and 86.
31 *Ibid*, 78.
32 *Ibid*, 92.
33 *Ibid*, 95–6.
34 *Ibid*, 105.
35 Shaunnagh Dorsett and Shaun McVeigh, 'Questions of Jurisdiction' in Shaun McVeigh (ed.), *Jurisprudence of Jurisdiction* (Oxon: Routledge-Cavendish, 2007) 3.
36 Thomas Hobbes, *Leviathan* (J C A Gaskin ed., Oxford: Oxford University Press, 1996).
37 Richard Tuck, 'The "Modern" Theory of Natural Law' in Anthony Pagden (ed.), *The Languages of Political Theory in Early-Modern Europe* (Cambridge: Cambridge University Press, 1987) 99, 118.
38 *Ibid*, 87.

39 *Ibid*, 222.
40 Daniela Coli, 'Hobbes's Revolution' in Victoria Kahn, Neil Saccamano and Daniela Coli (eds), *Politics and the Passions, 1500–1850* (Princeton and Oxford: Princeton University Press, 2006) 75.
41 UN Secretary General Kofi Annan, *In Larger Freedom: Towards Development, Security and Human Rights for All*, 135, UN Doc A/59/2005 (21 March 2005), available at http://www.un.org/largerfreedom/contents.htm.
42 On this conception of the relation between a transcendental form of life and biological life, see Timothy Campbell, '*Bios*, Immunity, Life: The Thought of Roberto Esposito' in Roberto Esposito, *Bios: Biopolitics and Philosophy* (trans Timothy Campbell, Minneapolis: University of Minnesota Press, 2008) vii, xv.
43 Thomas Hobbes, above note 36, 113.
44 *Ibid*, 113–14 (on the need for a common power to keep people in awe). The US military doctrine of 'shock and awe' or 'rapid dominance' was developed by Harlan Ullman and James Wade in 1996, and officials in the US armed forces used the language of 'shock and awe' to describe their strategy in invading Iraq. See further Harlan K Ullman and James P Wade, *Shock and Awe: Achieving Rapid Dominance* (National Defense University, 1996) xxiv, stating: 'The aim of Rapid Dominance is to affect the will, perception, and understanding of the adversary to fit or respond to our strategic policy ends through imposing a regime of Shock and Awe'.
45 Thomas Hobbes, above note 36, 111.
46 Noel Malcolm, *Aspects of Hobbes* (Oxford: Clarendon Press, 2002) 228.
47 See generally Anne Orford, 'International Law and the Making of the Modern State: Reflections on a Protestant Project' (2008) 3(1) *In-Spire: Journal of Law, Politics and Societies* 5–11, available at http://www.in-spire.org/archive/vol3–no1/ao21072008_international_law.pdf
48 Gaines Post, *Studies in Medieval Legal Thought: Public Law and the State, 1100–1322* (Princeton: Princeton University Press, 1964) 569, commenting that nowhere could the medieval State or royal government 'exact that obedience of subjects which is generally obtained by the State in the twentieth century'.
49 Immanuel Kant, 'The Metaphysics of Morals ' in H S Reiss (ed.), *Kant: Political Writings* (Cambridge: Cambridge University Press, 1991) 131, 143.
50 Immanuel Kant, 'On the Common Saying: "This May be True in Theory, But it Does Not Apply in Practice"' in H S Reiss (ed.), *Kant: Political Writings* (Cambridge: Cambridge University Press) 61, 80.
51 *Ibid*.
52 *Ibid*, 81.
53 Immanuel Kant, above note 49, 144.
54 GFW Hegel, *Hegel's Philosophy of Right* (trans T M Knox, Oxford: Oxford University Press, 1952) 285.
55 Thomas Hobbes, above note 36, at 222.
56 See generally Adam Smith and Edwin Cannan, *Lectures on Justice, Police, Revenue and Arms* (Oxford: Clarendon Press, 1896); Michel Foucault, *Security, Territory, Population: Lectures at the Collège de France 1977–1978* (trans Graham Burchell, Hampshire: Palgrave MacMillan, 2007).
57 Carl von Clausewitz, *On War* (trans Michael Howard and Peter Paret, Princeton: Princeton University Press, 1976).
58 *Behrami and Behrami v. France*, App. No. 71412/01, *Saramati v. France, Germany, and Norway*, App. No. 78166/01, European Court of Human Rights Grand Chamber, Decision on Admissibility (31 May 2007).
59 *Ibid*, 146.
60 *Ibid*, 149.
61 *Ibid*, 43.

62 *Ibid*, 151.
63 *Ibid*, 100.
64 Jürgen Habermas, *America and the World (Interview)*, 3.3 LOGOS (2004), available at http://www.logosjournal.com/issue_3.3/habermas_interview.htm.
65 Jacques Derrida, *The Post Card: From Socrates to Freud and Beyond* (trans Alan Bass, Chicago: The University of Chicago Press, 1987) 56.
66 Didier Fassin, 'Humanitarianism as a Politics of Life' (2007) 19 *Public Culture* 499.
67 *Ibid*, 513.
68 Martti Koskenniemi, 'The Silence of Law/The Voice of Justice' in Laurence Boisson de Chazournes and Philippe Sands (eds), *International Law, the International Court of Justice and Nuclear Weapons* (Cambridge: Cambridge University Press, 1999) 488.
69 *Ibid*, 508–9.
70 Brigadier General Thomas F Farrell, quoted in John Whittier Treat, *Writing Ground Zero: Japanese Literature and the Atomic Bomb* (Chicago and London: The University of Chicago Press, 1995) x.
71 Hersch Lauterpacht, 'The Problem of the Revision of the Law of War' (1952) *British Year Book of International Law* 382.
72 For a more detailed discussion of this incident, see Anne Orford, 'The Destiny of International Law' (2004) 17 *Leiden Journal of International Law* 441.
73 US Secretary of State Colin L Powell, *Remarks to the United Nations Security Council*, 5 February 2003, available at http://www.state.gov/secretary/rm/2003/17300pf.htm.
74 Maureen Dowd, 'Powell without Picasso', *The New York Times*, 5 February 2003: A27.
75 On the 'double veils of cloth and flags', see Miriam Hansen, 'Statement on Critical Inquiry in the 21st Century', *Critical Inquiry* Editorial Board Meeting, Public Symposium, 11 April 2003, available at http://criticalinquiry.uchicago.edu/issues/v30/30n2.Hansen.html.
76 Maureen Dowd, above note 74.
77 Jacques Derrida, 'Force of Law: The "Mystical Foundation of Authority"' (1990) 11 *Cardozo Law Review* 921, 993.
78 *Ibid*, 991–3.
79 The phrase 'terror bombing' is taken from Herschel B Chipp, *Picasso's Guernica: History, Transformations, Meanings* (Berkeley: University of California Press, 1988) 156.
80 Jacques Derrida, above note 77, 963.
81 John Berger, 'Success and Failure of Picasso' in Ellen C Oppler (ed.), *Picasso's Guernica* (New York: W W Norton, 1988) 267, 271.
82 Jacques Derrida, above note 77, 943.
83 See particularly George L Steer, 'The Tragedy of Guernica: Town Destroyed in Air Attack', *The Times*, 28 April 1937, reprinted in Ellen C Oppler (ed.), *Picasso's Guernica* (New York: W W Norton, 1988) 160, 161 ('In the form of its execution and the scale of the destruction wrought, no less than in the selection of its objective, the raid on Guernica is unparalleled in military history'.)
84 On the figure of the fallen warrior as a reference to the eleventh-century manuscript of the *Apocalypse of Saint-Sever*, see Ellen C Oppler, 'Introductory Essay' in Ellen C Oppler (ed.), *Picasso's Guernica* (New York: W W Norton, 1988) 45, 92.
85 Michel Leiris, 'Faire-part' in Ellen C Oppler (ed.), *Picasso's Guernica* (trans Ellen C Oppler, New York: W W Norton, 1988) 210.
86 José Bergamín, 'Naked Poetic Truth', in Ellen C Oppler (ed.), *Picasso's Guernica* (New York: W W Norton, 1988) 201, 202.
87 Martti Koskenniemi, above note 68, 508.
88 *Ibid*, 510.

89 Michel Foucault, *Society Must Be Defended: Lectures at the Collège de France* (trans David Macey, London: Penguin, 2003) 246–7.

90 On the relationship of the theological concepts of sin, salvation and redemption to the internationalist projects of development and state-making, see further Jennifer Beard, *The Political Economy of Desire: International Law, Development and the Nation State* (Oxon: Routledge-Cavendish, 2007).

3   Gendered humanitarianism

Reconsidering the ethics of war

Kimberly Hutchings

Introduction

For some time there has been a growing literature focused on deconstructing the concept of the 'human' in the ideas of 'human rights' and of 'humanitarianism' that have played such a significant part, both rhetorically and practically in post-cold-war politics.[1] There has also been the growth of a major literature focused specifically on the rights and wrongs of military humanitarian intervention,[2] including feminist work addressing humanitarian legitimations of war.[3] This chapter draws on these literatures in order to examine the assumptions that enable ethical humanitarianism, philosophically and in practice, especially when it takes a violent form. In particular, I am interested in how assumptions about moral authority and agency necessary for humanitarian ethics are underpinned by gendered discriminations of the human. And in the implications that, from a feminist perspective, follow from challenging those assumptions, for humanitarianism in general and humanitarian war specifically.

Of all of the developments in international politics in the past twenty years it is humanitarianism (a category that increasingly encompasses a range of practices from emergency aid to peacekeeping and war making) that apparently relies most clearly on a universal conception of the human, since it is the violation of the human as such that triggers the requirement for a humanitarian response. As many scholars have argued however, if we examine the humanitarian script, we find not a notion of the 'human' as such, but rather sets of criteria through which the simply 'human' are differentiated from other sorts of human. In the first two sections of what follows, I will argue that this is true across the range of humanitarian practices, from famine relief to military intervention for humanitarian purposes, but that it becomes particularly stark and consequential in the case of military humanitarian intervention, where the script of a politics of rescue meets the script of just war. I will argue that the only way in which the script of military humanitarian intervention can be sustained is by reproducing differences between people, most reliably through the naturalising effects of familiar gendered narratives. These gendered narratives replay, and thereby embed and reinforce, understandings of moral authority and moral agency that permit a way of thinking about war that keeps it at a distance. On these accounts the 'just warrior' remains untouched by war, even as he makes war.

The gendered humanitarian script poses particular problems for feminist theorists seeking to establish legitimate grounds for war making. In the final section of the chapter, I turn to examine feminist engagements with the ethics of war that are premised on a scepticism about the sanitised relation to violence suggested by the 'just warrior', but that simultaneously remain self-consciously 'in touch' with collective political violence as part of a repertoire of possible responses to injustice. Many feminists have argued that the gendered presuppositions of war make feminism incompatible with any kind of ethical legitimation of war, however humanitarian.[4] In contrast, theorists such as Jean Elshtain and Laura Sjoberg, from different perspectives, argue for the possibility (or necessity) for feminists to engage in ethical discrimination between different kinds of violence.[5] Both thinkers are critical of the gendered narratives that work to leave us untouched by war. But they see feminist pacifists as effectively colluding with the humanitarian fairy story, by placing themselves as outside of, or as uncontaminated by, the existence of political violence. I will suggest, however, that in their opening up of ethical thinking to the wounds of war, there is an ever present danger of reinventing the (gendered) fairy tales through which it has traditionally been justified. The acknowledgement of complexity and ambiguity is always in tension with nostalgia for the moral authority and agency of the maximally human, and the asymmetric relation between hero, victim and villain. In this respect, the work of Elshtain and Sjoberg sits more or less uneasily between the humanitarian script and the insights of feminist ethics.

The purpose of the following argument is not to make a case that is either for or against humanitarianism. In relation to humanitarianism in general, I argue that the category of the 'human' is one that is always embedded in narratives and practices that belie its pretensions to universality and neutrality, and that simplify and thereby distort the ethical stakes of humanitarian action for both 'rescuer' and 'victim'. In relation to military humanitarian intervention I argue that for feminists in particular the ethical legitimation of such actions poses deep problems. Awareness of these problems does not resolve them, but it does point us to the need to incorporate the ethically weighty consideration of the practice and experience of war into our *ad bellum* and *in bello* judgments about it. Moreover, any serious touching of war as a practice and experience implies a need to rethink predominant accounts of moral authority and moral agency in humanitarian ethics and politics.

The ethics of humanitarianism

Peter Singer's article, 'On famine, affluence and morality', exemplifies humanitarianism as a universal doctrine, premised on the moral significance of the human as such.[6] Inspired by the famine in East Bengal, Singer made a trenchant and straightforward utilitarian argument as to why affluent people in the developed world were morally obliged to contribute to famine relief even up to the point of marginal utility. In doing so, Singer cut through a range of traditional moral arguments that claimed that moral obligations of charity did not hold towards distant strangers, asserting that the unnecessary suffering and death of humans per se triggered obligations on all other humans to do something about it. Singer's argument, then, appeared to rely solely on a universal conception of the human. On his account any human undergoing unnecessary suffering and death prompts the moral requirement for help from any other human. On examination, however, there is still a differentiation in Singer's argument between the human element of the ethical relation who either helps or does not help and the 'simply' human element that requires or demands help. The latter is recognisable because of his or her 'unnecessary' (that is to say preventable) suffering and danger, but also because of his or her inability to help his or herself. This kind of 'human' is the residual core of what it means to be human, the core to which the former human, if necessary, is obliged *almost* to strip himself or herself, if he or she is to respond to their own and the other's humanity adequately.

In order for Singer's argument to be persuasive, we not only have to be convinced by his account of the moral implications of unnecessary human suffering and death, but also of a relation between humans characterised by agency and power on the one hand and the absence of agency and power on the other. In addition to this there are two further assumptions implicit in the argument. First, that the origins of the famine are irrelevant to the morality of the situation. This is underlined in Singer's famous analogy between the obligation to provide famine relief and the rescuing of a child from drowning in a puddle. According to Singer, refusing to give famine relief is the moral equivalent of leaving the child to drown because the act of saving might get your clothes wet. The fact that this is a child means that we do not take his or her agency seriously when it comes to the question of how he or she got into the puddle in the first place, as well as the question of whether she or he has the ability to get out. Second, that the capacity to act of the affluent is linked to a means that we know will work, and that will neither preserve the status quo nor make the famine worse. The moral authority of the injunction to act is grounded in a high level of certainty about the efficacy of the action and the technical competency of the actor.

Singer's argument was powerfully made, and it provoked and continues to provoke a range of responses in relation to the ethics of humanitarian aid. If we look at these arguments we find that they tend to separate into three kinds. There are those that share Singer's utilitarian assumptions but argue that implications of utilitarian analysis are different, most notoriously in the argument that actually it would maximise the limitation of human suffering if the starving were allowed to die, and therefore limit unsustainable population growth.[7] Second, there are those that essentially agree with his analysis but ground the moral significance of human beings differently, often in a deontological account of fundamental human rights or human needs. In the case of rights-based arguments, the starving have had their rights violated and the affluent have a responsibility to respond to that violation, on some accounts not solely because they have the capacity to aid but also because they are partially responsible for that violation.[8] In the case of needs-based arguments, the affluent have a strict obligation to do something about the starving, whether they have deliberately contributed to the harm done or not.[9] The third kind of response challenges Singer's universalism, deploying a range of arguments to show that the relation between the affluent and the starving should not be read as analogous to the child in the puddle, perhaps because the responsibility for the starvation historically lies elsewhere, or the starving have an agency which the child/puddle analogy denies, or because the distance (geographical, cultural, political) between the affluent and the starving is morally salient on contractualist or communitarian grounds.[10] The impact of these arguments is not necessarily to deny the 'human' as a category altogether, but it is to suggest that the humanitarian relation only holds where we can be sure that the object of humanitarian help does not share either the capacity or responsibility of the helper. The 'human' in humanitarianism remains defined as a relationship between the fully human (knowledgeable, capable adult) and the residually or potentially human (ignorant, incapable child).

The above discussion attempts to make the point that even within the philosophical discussion of the ethics of humanitarianism, discrimination between modes of being human is essential. Humanitarianism is inherently relational and requires criteria for distinguishing between the human as helper and the human as helped. At the philosophical level this involves differentiating between degrees of responsibility and agency, which is in turn linked to the degree and immediacy of suffering and need. But of course, humanitarianism is not just an ethical position, it is a policy and a practice, one which, following Singer, seeks to respond to human suffering, simply on the grounds that it is human suffering. In putting this philosophy into practice, there therefore need to be ways in which human suffering as such can be distinguished from other kinds. The clues as to how this can be done are already there in the philosophical debates provoked by Singer's article in which the humanitarian call is located in those humans that are neither responsible for their plight nor able to do anything about it, and whose situation is capable of being addressed by the actions of others. But how do we know who these people are?

The answer, it would seem, is self-evident: these are the people displaced by the earthquake, by crop failures, by war, gathered in makeshift camps and shanty towns; their desperation speaks for itself. When it comes to the practical implementation of any humanitarian policy, however, suffering cannot just be taken to speak for itself, it has to be spoken for by a range of governmental and nongovernmental agencies that articulate the plight of the suffering to the institutional and individual actors who are deemed to be in a position to do something about it. This discourse has to construct the two dimensions of the humanitarian relation through entrenching a series of discriminations. One such discrimination is between purely human suffering and other kinds of suffering, since it is only with the assurance that the people in question are purely human (essentially innocent and incapable) that the claim that this is humanitarian aid becomes legitimate. This sets up a necessary boundary between 'deserving' and 'undeserving' recipients. At the other end of the humanitarian relation, other sorts of discrimination are at work: ones that separate out humanitarian givers from other kinds of powerful actors, those contributing for humanitarian purposes as opposed to acting in their own self-interest, those that have perpetrated the problem as opposed to those who will resolve it, or simply those who have the technical know-how and resources as opposed to those who don't.

The line drawn between humanitarian aid and other kinds of aid may be blurred by all sorts of considerations. Sometimes these relate to the causes of humanitarian crisis, sometimes to the length of time that the crisis has continued, the actions of either helper or helped, or the broader implications for the political context in which the humanitarian crisis unfolds. For example, if the crisis is the result of war (as is often the case), humanitarian aid can be seen as sustaining the conflict or benefiting one side or the other, perhaps including those who have done most to bring the crisis about. No donor wants to see their aid as a reward for violence or as the means by which dictators are kept in power. To count as humanitarian it needs to relate to the human as such, to be moral rather than political. Given that no situation of humanitarian crisis is without these kinds of complexities, humanitarian agencies need a language of humanitarianism through which they can link the objects of their help to a residual (and unthreatening) humanity (Singer's child), and the helpers to a fully fledged, powerful conception of humanity (Singer's adult). One of the most reliable ways of doing this is to foreground those recipients of aid that exemplify that residual and unthreatening humanity in Western thought, archetypally, the sick, the old and 'women and children'.

> Then a close-up of a baby – a tiny body, but a large head, and its mouth open wide in a silent cry. It is held close to its mother's face. She shields it with a cloth that drapes them both, drawing it to her and looks down. The infant's silent anguish, eyes closed, mouth wide, screaming, continues. Finally the mother tries to nurse it.[11]

As Edkins points out in her discussion of the coverage of the Ethiopian famine in 1984–5, even at the time there were many protests at the construction of the Ethiopians as pure 'victims' and the West as pure 'rescuers'. Since then, the academic debate surrounding emergency aid has increasingly sought to disrupt this simple binary, and practices and policies surrounding emergency aid have become increasingly sensitive to the political complexities of the contexts of such aid operations, and to the ways in which aid itself may contribute to creating and sustaining situations of emergency need.[12] However, as Edkins also points out, even as experts and technocrats challenge the idea that you can treat famine as a 'natural' disaster, if they are to preserve the meaning of humanitarian aid then they have to reinvent the humanitarian relation, in which the helper is defined by their capacity, and the helped by their incapacity, to address the sources of suffering.

The politics of rescue needs ways of cutting through the complexity and ambiguity of actual humanitarian crisis in order to establish distinctions between the innocent and guilty, victims and heroes. We can see this, as much as anything, in the reluctance of publics to accept that humanitarian workers themselves might need to be paid or to have their work in the field supported by bureaucracies. Organisations such as Oxfam are only able to retain their moral authority by affirming their actions are uncontaminated by interests, and that they have the knowledge and capacity to identify and rectify humanitarian wrongs. All of this is rendered plausible through gendered discriminations between rescuer and victim, autonomy and vulnerability, control and chaos. In the following section, I examine how the discriminations of the human that are embedded in the ethics of humanitarianism become intensified when humanitarianism turns to violence, where the discourse of a politics of rescue meets the discourse of just war.

Military humanitarianism

Humanitarianism originated as a response to the sufferings of those affected by war (often dated back to the founding of the Red Cross in 1863). The idea of military humanitarianism, although arguably foreshadowed in imperial 'civilisational' interventions in the nineteenth century, has only recently been recognised as a potentially legitimate, or even required, policy option for states and the international community. It brings together practices that have traditionally been seen as distinct into a new, hybrid practice that is both humanitarian and war. There are of course those who would deny the existence of 'humanitarian intervention' as an actual phenomenon – regarding the discourse of humanitarianism rather as an ideological disguise for the pursuit of straightforward national or sectional, elite interests. Within this chapter, however, I treat humanitarian intervention on its own terms as being, at least in part, about the pursuit of justice.

My interest is in the relation between the moral script of humanitarianism and the moral script of 'just war' into which, as a practice of war, military humanitarianism is inserted both by its proponents and opponents. Since scholars started to pay attention to the theory and practice of military humanitarian intervention in the 1990s, many commentators have pointed to its gendered dimensions, from the discourses through which it is described and legitimated, to the ways in which it should be carried out, to the nature of its aims, to its short- and long-term effects.[13]

The idea that just war thinking is a heavily gendered script is now well established in feminist and non-feminist scholarship. The classic statement of this gendering can be found in Elshtain's *Women and War*,[14] which demonstrated in detail how the discourses through which war has been legitimated in Western culture are premised on the division between 'just warrior' and 'beautiful soul', chivalrous protector and vulnerable victim, regardless of the actual roles played by men and women in collective violence. The just warrior/beautiful soul duality is constituted and maintained as mutually reinforcing through its inter relation with another gendered distinction between just (civilised – controlled masculinity) and unjust (barbarian – hyper-masculinity) warriors, the latter providing the requisite threat from which the beautiful souls must be protected. Scholars, such as Kinsella have shown how in the refinement and institutionalisation of Christian just war principles in Europe from the seventeenth century onwards, the distinction between legitimate and non-legitimate targets in war, traditionally that between the 'innocent' and the 'guilty' was stabilised by using sex/gender as a marker.[15] Whilst the borders between innocent and guilty, child and adult or sick and well were shifting, uncertain, not always easily observable, the bound-ary between male and female was presented as static and obvious. Some clear demarcation was necessary to sustain the distinction between Christian and bar-barian warfare, and that between male and female bodies became exemplary. In twentieth-century efforts to codify and reinforce the distinction between combat-ant and non-combatant, fighter and civilian, again the distinction between male and female bodies became crucial to 'in bello' justice. To the extent, as Carpenter argues, that the idea of a male civilian has become a kind of blind spot in both military and humanitarian thinking.[16]

If we take the main principles of just war: legitimate authority; just cause; proportionality *ad bellum*; proportionality and discrimination *in bello*, we can trace a gendered politics in relation to each in which the just warrior, his barbarian other and the beautiful soul play their appointed parts. However, in humanitarian intervention these archetypes become particularly clear, because of a mutual rein-forcement between the two discourses. The moral requirement to rescue is now compounded by the fact that someone is actively trying to push the child into the puddle. Both the vulnerability of the victim and the requirements on the rescuer are amplified by the addition of an evil perpetrator to the plot, which has been referred to as the 'fairy story' implicit in military humanitarianism.[17]

In his work on humanitarian intervention, Wheeler boils down the relevant just war criteria to just cause (supreme humanitarian emergency), last resort (neces-sity), proportionality (means should be proportional to ends) and probability of success (positive humanitarian outcome).[18] This slimmed down version of just war theory, involves dropping those categories from traditional just war theory, such as 'legitimate authority', 'just intention' or 'comparative justice', through which the gendered plot of just war might be disturbed. For example, 'legitimate authority' muddies the waters of the humanitarian plot because, under current international law, there can be just warriors that behave illegitimately (make illegal interventions), and barbarian actors that are legitimate (oppressive states) – thus blurring the gendered lines of, for instance, the distinction between the state as the legitimate user of controlled violence (over which it has a monopoly) as opposed to the terrorist organisation, the illegitimate user of uncontrolled vio-lence (to which it has no right). 'Just intention' is likewise potentially disruptive of just war certainties, because the idea of mixed motivations undermines the clarity of the 'just warrior' category – how could he be just if he was also acting to increase his own power as a barbarian warrior would? 'Comparative justice' traditionally calls upon parties to war to be aware of the fact that there can be right on both sides, or at least that, not being God, neither side can guarantee the cer-tainty of their own justice. But this is the most problematic criterion (guideline) of all for the purposes of humanitarian intervention, since the just cause is premised on a certainty of injustice, in which it could not be possible for both sides to be just warriors, or even to think of themselves in those terms.

I would suggest, therefore, that in humanitarian intervention we get a kind of distillation of the gendered just war plot, stripped of possible ambiguities, and reliant on simple assumptions about the moral authority and moral agency of the just warrior and the innocence and incapacity of the 'beautiful soul', which in turn set up what it means to act morally in the face of injustice, the villainous third party. As with the representation of the Ethiopian famine referred to earlier, no one could ever take this as an accurate account of the complex politics of any humanitarian emergency, which raises the question of why the plot remains ethically convincing. Clearly one reason is that as with the earlier example, the account of moral authority and agency involved here is sustained by gendered binaries that enable clear-cut distinctions between reason and emotion, autonomy and vulnerability, control and anarchy, rescuer and victim.

The moral authority of the humanitarian just warrior relies on the same kinds of moral self-certainty that Singer articulates in his account of the ethics of famine relief in terms of knowledge of the natures of, and relation between, rescuer and victim, and in terms of confidence in his own capacity and technical competence. This moral self-certainty *necessarily* requires that not all humans share the knowledge, the capacities or the goodness of the just warrior. As a moral actor, he is rational, autonomous and self-disciplining. This rationality and autonomy underpin a capacity for heroic action, in which he stands up for the right in the face of others' evil or indifference ('here I stand I can do no other'). Within this account of moral authority and agency, moral humility and emotion are marginalised, in part through the disconnection between the just warrior and the differently human. Those uncertain of what to do or incapable of action by definition cannot be just warriors. And it is only because not everyone is human in the same way that the just warrior is able to be a humanitarian, and discriminate between the inhuman (perpetrator) and the residually human (victim). The same qualities of rationality and autonomy that ground moral authority, also underpin moral agency as the capacity to act, for moral purposes, in a way that instantiates the good in the world through controlled and controllable means. Although Singer's moral actor does not engage in violence, he does presume the reliability and neutrality of the techniques through which suffering should be addressed, and this presumption is bound up with the moral actor as both knowledgeable and in control. The just war theory script introduces humanitarianism to violence as a technique, but the conviction of the capacity of the moral agent to direct and control the means and outcomes of action is already entrenched in the humanitarian script, even in the face of the mass of evidence of the failure of violence to deliver its aims. Moreover, the humanitarian hero remains himself unaffected by the violence he employs, the practice and experience of killing and injuring in no way compromises either his authority or his agency.

Feminists touching war

One of the most significant dimensions of feminist ethical and political thought over the past thirty years has been its challenging of the conception of moral authority and agency embedded in the script of humanitarian ethics. Most notably in the ethics of care, feminist moral philosophers have disrupted the discriminations that underpin the fiction of the rational and autonomous moral agent, not solely because of the gendered politics that this fiction is sustained by and reproduces but also because, feminists argue, it misrepresents the conditions of possibility of moral authority, agency and action.[19] A feminist account of moral agency premised, in Bar On's words, on 'attentiveness to life as it is lived and experienced',[20] problematises the humanitarian script because it undermines the clarity of the distinction between the fully and the residually human. The discriminations that enable Singer's humanitarian actor and the just warrior in military humanitarian intervention to act rightly cannot be maintained if the difference and separation between them and the victim and perpetrator does not stand up to scrutiny. Challenging this difference/separation not only disrupts the rescuer/victim and rescuer/perpetrator distinctions, but also the distinction between the means and outcomes of action, given that the latter is only sustained by the myth of autonomy that full humanity requires.

Humanitarian arguments provided a distinct strand of justification for both of the US-led wars in Afghanistan and Iraq. In both cases the enemy regime was presented not only as a threat to others but also as an oppressor of its own population, in the case of Afghanistan in particular the population of women. Feminist responses to 9/11 and its aftermath, although predominantly critical, demonstrated how the question of the legitimacy of violence is contested within feminism.[21] From a feminist point of view, the imbrication of humanitarian war making in the reproduction of gendered hierarchies and dangerously hubristic accounts of moral authority and agency undermines claims to ethical legitimacy.[22] Feminists have argued that the practice of humanitarian violence requires an ethical orientation in tension with humanitarian goals, which give priority to the relief of suffering. In order to kill and injure, not only do soldiers (whether men or women) have to identify their enemy as killable, they have also to sustain a vision of their own just violence through gendered discriminations that reproduce and reinforce gendered relations of power. And the experience of violence, of both perpetrators and victims, is deeply transformative of the moral agent, leaving legacies of trauma and disconnection that persist, and potentially corrupt the heroism of the hero and the humanitarian outcome at which military action is directed.[23] In spite of this, however, feminists returning to re-think the ethics of humanitarian war have certainly not all come to a pacifist conclusion.

Elshtain is sometimes referred to as a 'conservative' feminist and her position has been highly contentious within the feminist community.[24] Nevertheless, her theoretical work has both shaped and been influenced by feminist ethical thinking about moral authority and agency. In her book *Just War Against Terror*, Elshtain argues in favour of the invasion of Afghanistan after 9/11.[25] One of the threads at work in the book is a humanitarian one, in which military action is, in part, justified by the good it will deliver not just to the 'West' but also to the people, women in particular, of Afghanistan. As the author of *Women and War* in which the gendered discriminations enabling war were deconstructed, Elshtain is clearly well aware of the gendered script of war. From a feminist point of view, therefore, her position post 9/11 seems to contradict her previous arguments. On examination, however, Elshtain's justification of military humanitarianism turns out to be closer to the insights of feminist critiques of humanitarian war than is initially obvious. For Elshtain it is those who assume that we can eradicate war from the arena of international politics that are premising their arguments on a humanitarian fairy tale. In an exchange with Anthony Burke, who had criticised her argument in *Just War Against Terror* as a justification of imperialist violence, Elshtain responds that whereas Burke lives in a world of moral clarity, based on clear binaries between good and bad, war and peace, her argument embraces moral ambiguity.[26] In effect, Elshtain is turning the feminist critique against the humanitarian moral script and its implications for moral authority and agency against what she calls the 'new utopianism' of humanitarian critics of post-9/11 US and NATO violence. In order to do this, she relies on a return to some of the aspects of traditional just war theory that disturb the straightforward binaries of humanitarianism. In contrast to the simplified version of just war theory put forward by those seeking to identify clear criteria of justification for humanitarian uses of force,[27] Elshtain argues for a revival of an older version of just war theory, in which moral ambiguities are assumed to be ineradicable. For Elshtain, just war theory provides a resource for practical reasoning in a world in which the actualities of political violence and injustice present us with 'hard' choices.[28] From this standpoint feminist pacifism and versions of liberalism that envisage a world of perpetual peace (Burke) are equally guilty of a refusal to touch the murky world of political conflict.

Elshtain invokes a classical (Augustinian) realist sensibility as the most appropriate frame within which to reason morally about collective violence for humanitarian ends in contexts of complexity and moral ambiguity. In contrast, Sjoberg's work takes a very different feminist turn, though equally one in which the justification of political violence is not automatically ruled out on feminist grounds. For Sjoberg, who is deeply critical of Elshtain's post-9/11 arguments, the appropriate feminist response to the ethical issues raised by war, including humanitarian war, is to articulate a distinctively feminist just war theory.[29] In *Gender, Justice and the Wars in Iraq*, she sets out a systematic rewriting of just war principles from a feminist perspective, using the Iraq wars from 1990 onwards as an illustration. 'I argue that, through empathy, care, and dialogue, feminisms can revise, rewrite, and revitalize the just war tradition to deal with the political conflicts of the twenty-first century'.[30]

What Sjoberg refers to as her 'feminist security ethic of empathetic cooperation' builds on aspects of the feminist ethic of care and claims to avoid the distorting detachment provided by fairy tale accounts of just war, including humanitarian intervention. One of Sjoberg's key arguments is to introduce the notion of 'human security' into just war theory.[31] By doing this she makes the individual's experience of threat and harm central to the meaning of war. This draws attention to ways in which war is experienced, by people on the ground before and after the conflict's supposed beginning and end; it also draws attention to injuries and harms that may not be the direct result of violent means. As Sjoberg points out, in criticising assumptions about non-combatant immunity: 'The humanitarian impacts of war are so far reaching that it is not possible to be *immune* to them'.[32] This undercuts the gendered discriminations that underpin justifications of humanitarian war as the protection of the innocent from harm.

Although Sjoberg argues that her feminist security ethic provides grounds for the moral condemnation of the recent US-led wars in Iraq, it does not condemn war as such. Rather it attempts to formulate principles that provide a way into thinking about the ethical legitimation of war that are fundamentally in touch with the gendered experience of what war is and does. In spite of their bitter political opposition, therefore, there are commonalities between the positions of Elshtain and Sjoberg. In both cases they claim a greater 'realism' about the actualities of political violence than can be found in either feminist pacifism or gendered humanitarian ethics. I suggest, however, that in spite of their best efforts to 'touch' war, neither of them fully succeeds in escaping from the humanitarian fairy tale.

In Elshtain's case, a revealing aspect of her exchange with Burke focuses on her identification with a particular superhero. Burke points to Elshtain's use of the idea of a 'Spider-Man' ethic, in which superpowers are understood to carry and be obliged to respond to wrongs in any part of the world. Elshtain corrects Burke's understanding of the use of this analogy on the grounds that unlike Superman, Spider-Man is a deeply conflicted superhero, who is tormented by 'tragic' choices every step of the way. In place of the straightforward hero of humanitarian intervention, Elshtain argues that powers engaging in humanitarian intervention are flawed and compromised: 'What a pity that Burke has not familarised himself with this existential and troubled hero!'[33] On reflection, however, even though Elshtain's vision of the humanitarian hero may be more nuanced than the identity of 'Superman', her position still mirrors standard aspects of the humanitarian fairy tale. In particular, this is because of the way in which we are still presented with a three-fold world of hero, victim and villain. Spider-Man may be a flawed and tormented character, but it is still in him that the capacity for both action and moral agency resides. He is also, of course, still a man. The script remains one that is thoroughly gendered and is difficult to render plausible in the absence of gendered discriminations that simplify and disambiguate the world of political violence.

Sjoberg goes much further than Elshtain in putting the role of 'victim' under scrutiny. Her revised criteria for just war theory engage in detail with the actualities of the experience of war, and directly challenge the clarity of distinctions on which Elshtain relies, for instance in relation to the principle of non-combatant immunity. In Sjoberg's case, however, it is difficult to see how the highly demanding criteria she sets out for just war could actually be met in a world in which political violence remains part of the repertoire of political action. A just war theory based on a feminist security ethic of empathetic cooperation would appear to require a world in which the gendered discriminations that underpin the legitimation of war were no longer being made. In this respect, Sjoberg does end up sharing a lot of ground with feminist pacifism, and from Elshtain's point of view embraces the fairy tale of a political violence without remainder. That is to say, the fairy tale that is crucial to legitimations of military humanitarianism in the first place.

Conclusion

Feminist critiques of the 'human' in humanitarian suggest that it is multiply illusory. There is no universal humanity in either the residual or the maximal versions of the human that are built into it, not just because the two categories of human are mutually exclusive, but more significantly because they are both politically loaded, gendered fictions. But if this is so, where does this leave us in practice? When it comes to military humanitarianism, the examples of Elshtain and Sjoberg, in different ways, suggest that attempts to rewrite humanitarian scripts without reference to these gendered fictions are fraught with difficulty. This raises the question of whether in seeking to touch war as a practice and experience, feminists necessarily return to a choice between realism, however 'tragic', on the one hand, and pacifism (in practice if not in theory) on the other. As Bar On notes, this is a troubling conclusion in a world in which violence is embedded and feminists cannot but desire 'a normative differentiation of violence into kinds'.[34] The question is whether it is possible to develop our ethical and political imaginations in such a way that the discriminate violence played out in the humanitarian script does not depend on gendered fictions of moral authority and agency, and does not work so as to reproduce a world in which political violence is the default mode of political struggle. At present there is little evidence to suggest that our imaginations are capable of stretching so far.

Notes

1 See V. S. Peterson, 'Whose Rights? A critique of the "givens" in human rights discourses', *Alternatives*, Summer 1990: 303–44; J. Butler, *Precarious Life: the powers of mourning and violence*, London: Verso, 2004; T. Carver, 'What is the "Human" in Humanitarian', paper delivered to the International Studies Annual Convention, March 1–5 2005.

2 See N. Wheeler, *Saving Strangers: humanitarian intervention in international society*, Oxford: Oxford University Press, 2000; A. Bellamy, 'Humanitarianism', Chapter 10 of *Just Wars: from Cicero to Iraq*, Cambridge: Polity Press, 2006; R. Belloni, 'The Trouble with Humanitarianism', *Review of International Studies*, 33 (3) 2007: 451–74.

3 See J. Elshtain, *Just War Against Terror: the burden of American power in a violent world*, 2nd edition, New York: Basic Books, 2004; 'Against the New Utopianism', *Ethics and International Affairs*, 19 (2) 2005: 91–5; L. Sjoberg, *Gender, Justice and the Wars in Iraq: a feminist reformulation of just war theory*, Oxford: Lexington Books, 2006; M. Denike, 'The Human Rights of Others: sovereignty, legitimacy, and "just causes" for the "war on terror"', *Hypatia: A Journal of Feminist Philosophy*, 23 (2), 2008: 95–121.

4 See B. Carroll, 'Feminism and Pacifism: historical and theoretical connections', in R. Pierson (ed.) *Women and Peace: theoretical, historical and practical perspectives*, London: Croom Helm, 1987; S. Ruddick, *Maternal Thinking: towards a politics of peace*, London: The Women's Press, 1990.

5 J. Elshtain, *Just War Against Terror: the burden of American power in a violent world*, 2nd edition, New York: Basic Books, 2004; 'Against the New Utopianism', *Ethics and International Affairs*, 19 (2) 2005: 91–5; L. Sjoberg, *Gender, Justice and the Wars in Iraq: a feminist reformulation of just war theory*, Oxford: Lexington Books, 2006.

6 P. Singer, 'Famine, Affluence and Morality', *Philosophy and Public Affairs*, 1 (3), 1972: 229–43.
7 See G. Hardin, 'Lifeboat Ethics: the case against helping the poor', in W. Aiken and H. Lafolette (eds) *World Hunger and Morality*, Upper Saddle River, NJ: Prentice Hall, 1996.
8 See for example T. Pogge, *World Poverty and Human Rights*, 2nd edition, Cambridge: Polity Press, 2008.
9 See for example O. O'Neill, 'Rights, Obligations and World Hunger', in F. Jimenez (ed.) *Poverty and Social Justice*, Tempe, AZ: Bilingual Press, 1987.
10 For examples of these kinds of arguments, which all problematise Singer's utilitarian perspective see M. Walzer, *Thick and Thin: moral argument at home and abroad*, Notre Dame: University of Notre Dame Press, 1994; J. Rawls, *The Law of Peoples*, Cambridge, MA: Harvard University Press, 1999; T. Nagel, 'The Problem of Global Justice', *Philosophy and Public Affairs*, 33 (2), 2005: 113–47.
11 J. Edkins, *Whose Hunger? Concepts of famine, practices of aid*, Minneapolis: University of Minnesota Press, 2000: 107–8.
12 Ibid: 129–52; M. Barnett and T. Weiss (eds) *Humanitarianism in Question*, Ithaca and London: Cornell University Press, 2008.
13 See C. Cockburn and D. Zarkov (eds) *The Post-War Moment: militaries, masculinities and international peace-keeping*, London: Zed Books, 2002; L. Sjoberg, *Gender, Justice and the Wars in Iraq: a feminist reformulation of just war theory*, Oxford: Lexington Books, 2006.
14 J. Elshtain, *Women and War*, New York: New York University Press, 1987.
15 H. Kinsella, 'Securing the Civilian: sex and gender in the laws of war', in M. Barnett and R. Duvall (eds) *Power in Global Governance*, Cambridge: Cambridge University Press, 2005.
16 R. C. Carpenter, '"Women and Children First": gender norms and humanitarian evacuation in the Balkans 1991–5', *International Organization*, 57 (Fall), 2003: 661–94.
17 R. Belloni, 'The Trouble with Humanitarianism', *Review of International Studies*, 33 (3) 2007: 451–74.
18 N. Wheeler, *Saving Strangers: humanitarian intervention in international society*, Oxford: Oxford University Press, 2000.
19 F. Robinson, *Globalizing Care: ethics, feminist theory and international relations*, Boulder, CO: Westview Press, 1999; L. Sjoberg, *Gender, Justice and the Wars in Iraq: a feminist reformulation of just war theory*, Oxford: Lexington Books, 2006; V. Held, *The Ethics of Care: personal, political, and global*, Oxford: Oxford University Press, 2006.
20 B-A. Bar On, 'Introduction: thinking about war', *Hypatia: A Journal of Feminist Philosophy* 23 (2): x.
21 F. Alloo *et al.*,'Forum: the Events of the 11th September and Beyond', *International Journal of Feminist Politics*, 4 (1), 2002: 95–113; B-A. Bar On *et al.*,'Forum on the War on Terrorism', *Hypatia: A Journal of Feminist Philosophy* 18 (1), 2003: 157–231; K. Hutchings, 'Simone de Beauvoir and the Ambiguous Ethics of Political Violence', *Hypatia: A Journal of Feminist Philosophy*, 22 (3), 2007: 111–32; B-A. Bar On, 'Introduction: thinking about war', *Hypatia: A Journal of Feminist Philosophy* 23 (2): x.
22 S. Ruddick, *Maternal Thinking: towards a politics of peace*, London: The Women's Press, 1990; L. Sjoberg, *Gender, Justice and the Wars in Iraq: a feminist reformulation of just war theory*, Oxford: Lexington Books, 2006.
23 F. Alloo *et al.* 'Forum: the Events of the 11th September and Beyond', *International Journal of Feminist Politics*, 4 (1), 2002: 95–113; D. Poe, 'Replacing Just War Theory with an Ethics of Sexual Difference', *Hypatia: A Journal of Feminist Philosophy*, 23 (2), 2008: 33–47.

24 Sjoberg offers a sustained feminist critique of Elshtain in L. Sjoberg, *Gender, Justice and the Wars in Iraq: a feminist reformulation of just war theory*, Oxford: Lexington Books, 2006.

25   J. Elshtain, *Just War Against Terror: the burden of American power in a violent world*, 2nd edition, New York: Basic Books, 2004.

26 J. Elshtain, 'Against the New Utopianism', *Ethics and International Affairs*, 19 (2) 2005: 95; A. Burke, 'Against the New Internationalism', *Ethics and International Affairs*, 19 (2), 2005: 73–89.

27 See N. Wheeler, *Saving Strangers: humanitarian intervention in international society*, Oxford: Oxford University Press, 2000.

28 J. Elshtain, 'Against the New Utopianism', *Ethics and International Affairs*, 19 (2) 2005: 92.

29 L. Sjoberg, *Gender, Justice and the Wars in Iraq: a feminist reformulation of just war theory*, Oxford: Lexington Books, 2006: 165–80.

30 Ibid: 15.

31 Ibid: 51.

32 Ibid: 101.

33 J. Elshtain, 'Against the New Utopianism', *Ethics and International Affairs*, 19 (2) 2005: 93.

34 B-A. Bar On, 'The Opposition of Politics and War', *Hypatia: A Journal of Feminist Philosophy*, 23 (2), 2008: 149.

4   Wars, bodies, and development

Brigitte M. Holzner[1]

As in the war that resulted in the break-up of Yugoslavia, armed conflicts and wars in Africa have a sad reputation for using sexual violence as a so-called weapon of war. Notably in Burundi, Liberia, Sierra Leone, Darfur, and Congo, there has been an epidemic of gender-based violence (GBV) ('In their own words', *Forced Migration Review* 2007: 47).[2]

During armed conflict, women and girls become the victims of rape and sexual violence, sexual slaves of male combatants and soldiers, so-called bush wives who perform domestic duties during the day and provide sexual services during the night. The rape and sexual abuse of women and girls as a strategy of war is used not only to demonstrate power and humiliate the enemy, but also to promote pregnancies to create new 'natives', or to intentionally infect them with HIV to physically weaken the enemy. Incidentally, peacekeepers of the United Nations, who are brought in to stop the fighting and protect civilians, also sexually abuse women and girls (United Nations General Assembly 2005; Lynch 2005; Cravero 2008; Crossette 2008). The rise in the trafficking of women or girls for sexual exploitation is also attributed to the presence of peacekeepers and humanitarian personnel, which raises the question of misogyny, the contempt and hatred of women, in the military culture.

As a response to the atrocities perpetrated on women and girls during armed conflict, and the human rights abuses committed by peacekeeping forces, the United Nations Security Council passed several resolutions regarding women, peace, and security (nr. 1325, 1820, 1888, 1889). In this chapter I describe and analyse these UN Security Council resolutions, asking what they have triggered, how they are used, what they can mean, and what their shortcomings are. I shall concentrate on some international responses to the resolutions, their impact on the national levels, and will conclude with a discussion of their potentials and shortcomings.

With regard to international politics I refer to the United Nations and the European Union, while regarding policy I address the spin-offs to research, action plans, conferences, training, and advocacy that the resolutions have given rise to. As a psychologist I am especially interested in stereotypes and mental frames, while as a development sociologist I am concerned about the securitization of the gender and development discourse. I shall first present the UN resolutions and then discuss their spin-offs. As examples, I use two war zones, Bosnia and Herzegovina, and Liberia, which are part of my work experience, in order to illustrate some of the complexities of war and how it is gendered in several ways. These examples help to show to what degree the UN resolutions reflect the dynamics of war and armed conflict.

Prelude one

Between 1992 and 1995 a war raged in Bosnia and Hercegovina (BiH), one of the former states of the Federal Republic of Yugoslavia. Serb and Croat forces attacked Bosniacs (Muslim Bosnians) for the purpose of creating mono-ethnic territories. Crimes like so-called ethnic cleansing through killing, eviction, and the destruction of villages were used to create areas without Bosniacs. Numerous women and girls were held in rape camps (Allen 1996), while men were kept in camps where they were reportedly sexually assaulted and castrated (United Nations 1992; Stiglmayer 1994; Zarkov 2007). Around 100,000 people lost their lives and 1.8 million people were displaced. The capital Sarajevo was under siege for three years, its inhabitants only surviving through aid packages from the United Nations. Although all ethnic groups suffered many casualties, Bosniac losses amounted to 66 per cent, followed by Serbs (25%), and Croats (8%). The remaining casualties were small numbers of Albanians and Romani people.

Near the town of Srebrenica in East Bosnia the United Nations with their protective forces UNPROFOR, consisting of a Dutch battalion (Dutchbat), created a 'safe area' where thousands of refugees sought some protection, albeit under dire circumstances as food and water were in short supply. In July 1995 a massacre occurred there: Serb forces entered the area and separated women and children under the age of 15 from the men at the factory site in Potocari. The women and children were transported by bus to various cities further north while more than 8,000[3] of the men were loaded onto trucks and taken away to be killed. Their corpses were thrown into 87 mass graves[4] (Zajovic *et al.* 2007: 164; Nuhanovic 2007; http://en.wikipedia.org/wiki/Srebrenica_massacre).

NATO finally intervened and peace negotiations were held in Dayton, Ohio, leading to the Dayton agreement that was signed by the Serbian President Slobodan Milošević, Croatian President Franjo Tuđman, and Bosnian President Alija Izetbegović. The Dayton agreement created the multi-ethnic state of Bosnia and Hercegovina, consisting of the Republica Srpska and the so-called Federation of Bosnia and Hercegovina, with altered territorial hegemonies of the ethnic groups.[5] Since then, foreign troops have been deployed to prevent new fighting, first the NATO-led IFOR (Implementation Force), taking over the forces of the UNPROFOR, then the Stabilisation Force (SFOR), and since 2004 the EU-led peacekeeping force (EUFOR). UNMIBH, the United Nations Mission in Bosnia and Herzegovina (1995–2002) was installed with a mandate to establish the rule of law. The country is still assisted by international organizations, administrators, and military forces in its governance, reconstruction, and community building, with strong powers being held by the Office of the High Representative.

The factory building where all this occurred has now been converted into a memorial site where photographs and some of the uncovered belongings of the murdered men are displayed: a comb, a button, a handkerchief, a picture of the family. Opposite the factory is the Srebrenica genocide memorial, where the names of more than 8,000 victims are engraved in a memorial wall.[6] There are graves with a stone and a name for those exhumed bodies that were at least 60 per cent complete so that they could be buried according to Muslim law. The identification of the dead bodies has taken much time because Serb forces later opened many graves, moving parts of the maimed corpses to secondary and tertiary graves in order to complicate their identification (Durnford 2005).

In the former Dutchbat quarters another type of memorial remains: remnants of Dutch and Serb soldiers' graffiti interspersed with some Serb words. In a small room on the ground floor the words SEX ROOM are written in big letters besides the door. In a drawing a tank with a red phallus for a canon takes aim at a naked woman from behind, depicting a pornographic fantasy of war and aggression against women. On a wall in a room on the upper floor of the Dutch camp there are also drawings of nude women in lascivious postures, and many rows of tallies: four vertical strokes crossed by a horizontal one, such as one finds on prison walls as a way of counting the days.[7]

Amongst the graffiti a few words are written: '*No teeth …? A mustache …? Smells like shit …? Bosnian girl!*' These words express the antipathy felt by Dutch soldiers[8] toward those whom they should protect. It is the girl's body that disgusts the soldiers and their words show no compassion for the misery she suffered during days of walking when she faced violence, rape, hunger, thirst. They also show no understanding of the lack of hygiene in the overcrowded refugee camp that had no water, food, shade, or medical services, or the daytime temperatures of 40 degrees that they endured. Eight years later, in 2003, the artist Sejla Kameric[9] used those words to reveal the racist-cum-sexist side of the Bosnian war, superimposing the words over a black and white photograph of herself to create a photomontage that has been reproduced on postcards, posters and billboards.

The prevalence of rape and sexual slavery in Bosnia during the war is well known. During this period there are also documented cases of UN soldiers who, far from helping the victims (mainly Muslim women held and controlled by Serbs), were clients and users of their 'services' (Stiglmayer 1994). After the war, reports mention the rise of the sex industry where the international forces of peacekeepers, police, private military forces, and professional and administrative workers used the sexual services of local and later of imported and often trafficked foreign women.[10]

Prelude two

The 14 years of armed conflict in Liberia, between 1989 and 2003, caused about 250,000 deaths in a country with a population of 3.5 million, and displaced over 2 million people. It destroyed the infrastructure, brought about deep poverty, vast unemployment, and left the population traumatized (Specht 2006: 15). Fighting started in 1989 when Charles Taylor, who had earlier lived in the United States,

Figure 4.1

(Sejla Kameric, Bosnian Girl, poster, 100 x 70 cm, 2003
Courtesy: Kontakt. The Art Collection of Erste Group)

overthrew president Samuel Doe and seized most of the country. In 1995 he was elected president, beating his opponent Ellen Johnson-Sirleaf, an economist at the World Bank. In 1997 fighting started again when two rebel groups, Liberians United for Reconciliation and Democracy (LURD) and the Movement for Democracy in Liberia (MODEL), took up arms and soon controlled most of the country. Charles Taylor's troops and various other rebel groups committed 'serious human rights abuses and war crimes (…) against civilians and especially against women and girls who constitute the major target of atrocities such as evictions, looting, killings, abductions, forced cannibalism, rape, other forms of sexual and gender-based violence'.[11] After a peace agreement in 2003, which forced Charles Taylor into exile in Nigeria, the United Nations Mission in Liberia (UNMIL) came in and disarmed about 100,000 ex-combatants from LURD, MODEL and the former government of Liberia. In 2005 Ellen Johnson-Sirleaf again ran for president and won. In the fragile post-conflict situation, president Johnson-Sirleaf has put some prominent, experienced women into crucial government and ministerial positions as well as appointing a female chief of police. Furthermore, the first all-woman battalion of peacekeepers, consisting of 100 Indian women, was deployed in Liberia.

Remarkably, during the war years an estimated 30–40 per cent of the fighting forces, approximately 25,000–30,000 combatants, were women and girls.

> The majority of women were forced to participate although it is also estimated that significantly more women opted to participate in the second conflict than in the first. They chose to take up arms to protect themselves from sexual violence, to avenge the death of family members, because of peer pressure, for material gain, and for survival. Women played roles as commanders, porters, spies, sex slaves, cooks and mothers.
>
> (Amnesty International 2008: 5)

Specht (2006) identifies several motives for women to join Liberia's fighting forces: being raped created a bond of solidarity between the women and girls, avenging the violence they had experienced, seeking protection from male combatants against other warring factions, escaping poverty and deprivation, and in some cases even the desire for some luxury items like 'red shoes', as the title of Specht's book indicates. Whereas non-combatant girls among the rebels had low status and could only achieve some status through a 'marriage' with a male combatant, those who entered battle achieved status and were even feared as strong soldiers (ibid.:12). The female combatants report wanting equality with men, and in a situation of armed conflict taking up arms is probably the only option to escape vulnerability and discrimination. 'Anger makes you brave', one of these women is quoted as saying (ICRC 2008: 18).

The unusual case of a woman called 'Black Diamond' gained a certain notoriety in the international media. She was a fierce combatant and the leader of an armed women's unit called the 'Women's Artillery Commandos', a rebel unit that fought with LURD (Liberians United for Reconciliation and Democracy). 'Black Diamond' is a young woman who was raped at the age of 15 and forced to watch her parents being killed. She then decided to take up arms and commanded a group of Liberian women rebels (Bardue 2004; BBC 2003; Taylor 2006[12]). She was respected for her aggressiveness and fearlessness, but young girl combatants in her unit also spoke of her kindness to them. In the looted building that was her command centre and where she often stayed, she sprayed the words 'No stupid man allow' on the wall, expressing her feelings about certain despised men (Carroll 2003).

Apart from the female combatants in Liberia, a strong and influential women's peace group called Women in Peacebuilding Network (WIPNET) also gained a reputation. This network was founded across religious, ethnic, and political lines by a social worker named Leymah Gbowee.

> Market sellers, students, farmers, professionals – women from all walks of life – marched daily in drenching rain and searing sun, often with their children on their backs, to demand the exit of their former leader, war criminal Charles Taylor, indicted by a special court in Sierra Leone, and to insist on an end to civil strife.
>
> (Woods and Veneklasen 2006: 1)

When peace talks finally started in Accra, members of WIPNET went to Ghana in order to influence the talks. Liberian women refugees joined them there. After weeks of talks among the warlords and members of the Taylor government, these women occupied the building where the negotiations were taking place, pressuring the delegates to come to a peace agreement (Paye-Layleh 2003). Their most effective strategy was to take off their dresses, and through their nakedness shame the men back to the negotiation table. As Leymah Gbowee, the initiator of the demonstrations explained, it is scandalous for a man to see a mother or elderly woman naked.[13] Maternal nudity expresses an ultimate vulnerability while at the same time it confers ultimate power, as the naked body becomes an invulnerable shield. Due to the pressure exerted by the women, members of WIPNET were invited to participate in the talks and thus helped shape the future the country. When a peace settlement was finally signed, Charles Taylor resigned and went into exile in Nigeria.[14] United Nations peacekeepers (UNMIL) came in to supervise disarmament and prevent new outbreaks of violence, and WIPNET continued to emphasize their responsibility for preventing violence against women and girls in the country.[15]

Features

These two cases of war and armed conflict, in Bosnia and Herzegovina, and in Liberia, have some features in common, and I have selected some for discussion.

In BiH there was the genocide of male victims, as well as weak international protection forces, contempt of women by the military as indicated by the Dutchbat camp graffiti, and peace negotiations imposed by foreign powers without the involvement of local women. The selected features of the armed conflict in Liberia include male and female combatants, a strong female peace movement, and graffiti that shows the contempt of men by armed women. Common to both countries is the huge number of internally displaced persons (IDPs). But whereas in BiH a kind of 'safe heaven', some protection from the attacking military was at least briefly provided, in Liberia this never existed. In both countries the systematic rape of and sexual assault against women has traumatized a huge number of people. Another major difference between the countries is their present leadership: whereas in BiH hardly any women came into government after the war (Lynne 2007: 25), in Liberia the government is largely 'feminised', with strong professional women in key ministries.

The atrocities against civilians during the wars of the 1990s and the first decade of the new millennium have raised the consciousness of the international community leading to debates in the UN Security Council. In the next section the results of these debates, formulated as resolutions that are the working mechanism of the Security Council, are presented, along with the spin-offs they have generated.

United Nations Security Council resolutions on women, peace, and security

In 2000 several members of the United Nations Security Council initiated debates concerning armed conflict: Namibia regarding women, peace, and security, Canada regarding the protection of civilians in armed conflict, and the Netherlands regarding children and focusing attention on human rights violations and needs of the population.[16] This was the first time that a link was made at the United Nations level between women and a gender perspective on the prevention and resolution of conflict, on building peace, and on post-conflict reconstruction. These actions lead to the adoption of the United Nations Security Council Resolution (UNSCR) nr. 1325 on Women, Peace, and Security on the 31st of October 2000.

The resolution is the result of cooperative efforts by members of the Security Council, notably Namibia, NGOs, and UNIFEM (Rehn and Johnson-Sirleaf 2002: 3). It relies on earlier resolutions and declarations like CEDAW (1979), the Beijing Platform of Action (1995), agreed conclusions of the Commission on the Status of Women (1998) and discussions in the Security Council.[17] The Windhoek Declaration (2000) in particular served as an inspiration for UNSCR 1325: In Windhoek in May 2000, the Government of Namibia hosted a seminar on 'Mainstreaming a Gender Perspective in Multidimensional Peace Support Operations', in which gender equality was demanded in all peace operations in order to enhance their effectiveness. The resulting Namibia Plan of Action demanded the participation of women in peace agreements and recruitment, and more leadership by women in decison-making structures and gender training, including a code of conduct for peacekeepers.

UNSCR 1325 (2000) in essence focuses on four dimensions of peace and security:

1   The protection of the human rights of women and girls before, during, and after armed conflict, and a consideration of the needs of women, girls, and female ex-combatants in IDP and refugee camps.
2   The participation of women at all levels of decision-making on all aspects of prevention, conflict settlement, and peace-building.
3   The inclusion of gender training for peacekeeping personnel.
4   Gender mainstreaming in the reporting and implementation systems of the United Nations relating to conflict, peace, and security.

Resolution 1325 calls upon the UN to increase female staff in peace operations and missions. It also requires the development of training materials concerning women's human rights, and a study on the impact of armed conflict on women and girls. Finally it demands a consideration of the role of women in peacebuilding and the gender dimensions of peace processes and conflict resolution. Member states are called upon to fund and provide support for gender-sensitive training and to end impunity, to prosecute those responsible for genocide and gender-based violence, and to make HIV/AIDS awareness training programmes available to military and civilian police. Parties in armed conflict should respect women's and girls' human rights and needs, protect them from gender-based violence, and enable women's participation in peace-building processes.

As an addition to UNSCR 1325, and in response to reports of misconduct by UN peacekeepers (UN General Assembly 2005), on the 19th June 2008 the UN Security Council adopted resolution 1820 that again addressed women and armed conflict, especially sexual violence against women. On the initiative of then US Secretary of State Condoleezza Rice this complementary resolution focused on rape as a war crime, as a crime against humanity, and as constituting an act of genocide. It urges states to impose a policy of zero tolerance, and to prosecute perpetrators and end their impunity. This resolution reiterates in stronger terms than UNSCR 1325 the necessity of protecting women and girls from acts of (sexual) violence during and after armed conflict, as well as the necessity of 'women's participation and full involvement in the prevention and resolution of conflicts'. It calls for stronger and clearer guidelines for UN peacekeepers to prevent sexual violence against civilians, and calls for more systematic and regular reporting on the issue.

UNSCR 1820 concentrates on the condemnation of sexual violence, on women and their empowerment, and on the necessity of making them part of conflict resolution and peacebuilding processes. It requires the recognition of their cause as legal subjects, and demands institutional assistance through the judicial and health sector, and the inclusion of a gender perspective in issues related to peace and security. UNSCR 1820 underlines that sexual violence as a tactic of war and 'as a security issue (…) deserves a security response' (UNIFEM Annual Report 2008–9: 5).

Late in September 2009 the USA proposed another addition to resolutions 1325 and 1820, and on the 5th of October 2009 Vietnam also tabled a new resolution regarding women, peace, and security. Resolution 1888 focuses on the establishment of a mechanism of accountability, e.g. through Women Protection Advisors, and the demand for a Special Representative on sexual violence in conflict[18]. Resolution 1889 requests that within six months there will be developed '*a set of indicators* for use at the global level to track implementation of its resolution 1325' (2000). Also, within 12 months there should be a 'written report to the Security Council addressing women's participation and inclusion in peacebuilding and planning in the aftermath of conflict' (UNSCR 1889 (2009, para 17 and 19). These recent additions are intended to overcome weaknesses in the implementation of resolution 1325, especially poor grassroots involvement in formal negotiations, and inadequate documentation and monitoring.

The UNSCRs on women, peace, and security exemplify the formula of the three Ps: prevention, protection, and participation. Protection of women and children, participation by women in the reconstruction of societies, i.e. peace negotiations and peacebuilding, and the prevention of violence against women and of illness (HIV/AIDS). Awareness of these matters is to be gained by training. With the inclusion of women in peace operations and missions, and the change of men's hearts and minds it is hoped that the three Ps will be realized. Basically, in all four resolutions we find two notions about women, namely 1) as victims and 2) as actors in peacebuilding. These notions acknowledge both suffering and agency, and recognize the rights and needs of women. The three Ps, together with the two notions, have inspired spin-offs in policy-oriented research, in national action plans, in conferences, in training, and in advocacy.

Selected spin-offs of UNSCR 1325, 1820, 1888, and 1889

Since its adoption, UNSCR 1325 has sparked a wide range of activities such as studies, conferences, and action plans. These various activities have not been conducted in isolation, but have on the contrary built on each other.

Policy-oriented research

Here I present two examples of policy-oriented research directly related to the resolution, one a United Nations study, and the other one conducted for the European Union.

1   The seminal 2002 study by Elisabeth Rehn and Ellen Johnson-Sirleaf,[19] *Women, War and Peace*, was commissioned by UNIFEM. This study, which provides an empirical body of data to the intentions of the resolution, covers the countries of Bosnia and Herzegovina, Cambodia, Columbia, the Democratic Republic of Congo, the Federal Republic of Yugoslavia (including Kosovo), Guinea, Israel, Liberia, the Occupied Palestinian Territories, Rwanda, Sierra Leone, and Somalia. It addresses violence against women, the situation of women refugees, health, HIV/AIDS, women and peace operations, organizing for peace, justice, media power, prevention and early warning, and reconstruction.

Each chapter ends with concrete recommendations. These include acknowledging violence against women as a war crime, and considering responding to women's needs and rights and to gender equality as integral to the processes of peace and transitional justice.

    They also address the special needs of women and girls as IDPs and of those who have been trafficked, with an emphasis on psychosocial support and reproductive health services for women affected by conflict. They advocate the strengthening of women's organizations and the participation of women, and promote the inclusion of gender experts in peace operations, training, staffing, and programmes. They appeal to national and international institutions to increase the number of women in senior positions in peace-related functions, fully implement women's rights through law enforcement, and to penalize perpetrators of violence. They conclude that more donor support, more information, more protection and participation, and better-trained personnel should mitigate the violation of the human rights of women and girls in situations of war and armed conflict.

This study had a great mobilizing effect. It resulted in conferences and the formulation of action plans regarding women, peace, and security, and ultimately led to the colloquium on women's empowerment, leadership development, international peace and security on the 7th and 8th March 2009. The friendship between E. Rehn and E. Johnson-Sirleaf became the basis for the cooperation between Liberia and Finland. By the time of the colloquium, E. Johnson-Sirleaf was president of Liberia and E. Rehn, now retired, had galvanized the Finnish political scene, resulting in Finland's president Tarja Halonen co-chairing the colloquium with E. Johnson-Sirleaf (see below).

2　The Slovenian presidency of the European Union during the first half of 2008 commissioned a study, co-financed by Austria and Germany, entitled 'Enhancing EU response to women and armed conflict with particular reference to development policy' (Sherriff with Barnes 2008). This study identified as key issues the ignorance of European institutions concerning the role of women in the prevention and resolution of conflict, despite international commitments like UNSCR 1325.

The study promoted the potential of a human security approach and a people-centred security sector reform (SSR), the importance of having access to a functioning and fair justice system, good gender equality-focused governance, the necessity of access to health and education for women, and the importance of economic development and livelihoods. Four policy issues are singled out in the study:

1　Sexual and gender-based violence (SGBV) requires a comprehensive approach 'beyond health to issues of security, livelihoods, justice and governance'.
2　Women's empowerment and improved accountability require strong women activists and women's organizations.
3　EU member states and conflict-affected countries need to develop national action plans for the implementation of UNSCR 1325.
4　Regional approaches to women and armed conflict that are more effective than purely nation-based initiatives.

(Sherriff with Barnes 2008: xii)

One major structural obstacle is the weak accountability, monitoring, and reporting mechanisms of the EU. Coherence among the EU policy for development, external relations, and defence, as well as continuity in interest and engagement for women and armed conflict are singled out as necessary follow-up mechanisms. For each of these issues several recommendations are made that target the whole of the EU architecture including the European Commission, the Directorate General for Development External Relations, Humanitarian Aid, Enlargement, and the European Council working groups on human rights and development, the European parliament, the European presidencies, the European Security and Defence Policy (ESDP), and Finances.

As a response to the study, and demonstrating some continuity between presidencies, the French EU presidency in December 2008 issued a 'Comprehensive approach to the EU implementation of the United Nations Security Council Resolutions 1325 and 1820 on women, peace, and security', which was adopted by the Council of the European Union (2008). It calls for the integration of external action and defence and development policies, and proposes a so-called three-pronged approach: political and policy dialogue, gender mainstreaming, and specific actions for empowerment. It foresees an annual discussion among EU member states concerning their plans of action, best practices, and difficulties in implementation. It also desires a platform for civil society from regions affected by conflict.

National action plans

One of the operational outcomes of UNSCR 1325 is the creation of national action plans (NAPs) for its implementation. These action plans are drafted by countries, especially those that deploy peacekeeping forces, as part of their external relations and development assistance. Several European countries have developed a NAP, including Denmark (2005), the United Kingdom (2006), Sweden (2006), Norway (2006), Austria (2007), The Netherlands (2007), Switzerland (2007), Finland (2008), Norway (2008), Spain (2008), Iceland (2008), Ireland (2008), Belgium (2009), and Portugal (2009).[20] The European NAPs are quite similar in structure and content. Most of them use multi-ministerial involvement, have consultations with civil society, and address lobbying in the EU. Some have indicators within a monitoring framework, and most focus on the areas of greater participation of women in peace missions, peacebuilding and reconstruction processes, as well as the training of peacekeepers, the protection of women and girls/children against especially sexual and gender-based violence. A few post-conflict countries also have NAPs for the implementation of UNSCR 1325. These include the Ivory Coast, Uganda, Timor Leste, and Liberia. BiH is also preparing such a plan.

The NAPs oblige governments and ministries to commit to concrete actions at the political level through lobbying at the UN and EU. They must prevent abuse by peacekeepers, and increase the peacekeepers' engagement in the protection of women and children where they are deployed. They must also prepare and support women in the processes of conflict resolution and peace. Refugees and IDPs in camps should get better facilities and protection from violence, and NGOs should broaden their work by linking development with the prevention of conflict and with reconstruction. It is important that those NAPs build in a mechanism to monitor and report, in order to guarantee their accountability to parliaments and civil-society groups.

Conferences

Since the adoption of UNSCR 1325 there have been numerous conferences on the topic. I shall limit myself to two[21]: the 2006 UNFPA-EC conference on sexual

violence in conflict and beyond, and the Liberia colloquium on women's empowerment, leadership development, international peace and security on the 7th and
8th March 2009.

More than 250 representatives from 30 countries attended the UNFPA-EC
symposium in Brussels. These included heads of UN agencies and NGOs, government representatives, representatives from criminal courts, the military and the
police, human rights and women's activists, field workers, and journalists. Many
women from conflict areas testified about atrocities and response mechanisms.[22]
A Brussels Call for Action was launched at the end of the conference, appealing
for a legal awareness of human rights and humanitarian law, the full participation of women, youth and vulnerable populations in the building of peace and in
reconstruction, in the formulation of plans of action, research on SGBV, and fore-
most, to 'prevent sexual and gender-based violence by promoting gender equity
and equality and the economic, social and political empowerment of women'.[23]

The international colloquium regarding women's empowerment, leadership
development, international peace and security, held in Monrovia on the 7th and
8th March 2009 also came under the heading of UNSCR 1325 and 1820. The
conceptualization of this international conference was a new one: it was organized in a post-conflict country that had experienced 14 years of brutal war that had
devastated its infrastructure and created huge problems of reconstruction and economic recovery. The conference assembled government leaders, representatives
of international organizations and of many non-governmental organizations. The
preparation of the conference was also unique. It was co-convened by Finland
and Liberia, with financial support from the European Commission and from
Denmark, Iceland, Ireland, Sweden, Spain, and Austria. Several international
organizations like the International Trade Commission (ITC), the International
Organization for Migration (IOM), UNIFEM, and UNDP, as well as some NGOs,
including the YWCA, Mary Robinson's Realizing Rights, and The Netherlands'
ICCO were involved as well. Together these organized a highly ambitious pro-
gramme, which, almost miraculously, was realized. The conference was opened
by seven heads of state, including E. Johnson-Sirleaf and President Tarja Halonen
of Finland as co-convenors, President Abdoulaye Wade of Senegal, President
Abdoulaye Kagame of Rwanda, Governor General Michelle Jean of Canada,
Prime Minister Luisa Dias Diago of Mozambique, First Vice President of Spain
Mara Teres Fernandez, and Vice president Ajaisatou Njie Saidy of Gambia.
Aisha Ghaddafi presented greetings from her father, then acting president of the
African Union. Video messages were broadcast from Germany's Angela Merkel,
Chile's Michelle Blanchelet, Suzanna Mubarak of Egypt, Israeli Tzipi Livni, and
Hillary Clinton of the US. The speeches all emphasized women's human rights,
the commitment to gender equality, the respect for UNSCR 1325 and 1820, the
importance of eradicating violence against women, and the necessity to have
women and their voices involved in the management of the current financial and
economic crisis. Curiously, and rather contradictorily, some of the speakers were
themselves authorities who had initiated war or armed conflict, or power holders
closely connected to authoritarian regimes.

During the conference, workshops were held on NAPs for UNSCR 1325, on the work of Truth and Reconciliation Commissions (TRCs), economic empowerment and decent work, migration, climate change, women in mediation, the empowerment of youth, and on women's leadership. A great ceremonial event was the launching of the Angie Brooks' International Centre for Women's Empowerment, Leadership Development, International Peace and Security as the follow-up to the colloquium. This centre will focus on research, training and advocacy, and will operate within a network structure linked to similar centres elsewhere. For instance, Maria Liberia-Peters, former president of the Netherlands Antilles, offered to cooperate with centres in the Caribbean region.

One outcome of the colloquium was the Monrovia Declaration with a Call to Action on women's empowerment, leadership development, international peace and security. Apart from calls for the immediate implementation of UNSCR 1325 and 1820, the Monrovia Declaration added the importance of women's leadership, women's economic participation, and the right to decent work, and, due to the influence of Finland, the mitigation of and adaptation to climate change to keep development sustainable.[24] The needs of and contributions by migrants and young people also received special attention. With these calls, the idea of peace and security is embedded in a framework of justice, global trade, as well as climate change. Remarkably, the image of the female victim is put aside, replaced by an image of women's leadership, strength, and work.

The Monrovia colloquium communicated a shift in feminist rhetoric: empowerment is important, but not enough. What matters now is women's leadership, although the direction of this leadership is as yet unclear. The commitment to gender equality continues, the desire for power is great, and history will show whether a guild of women in positions of power will be able to create a societal transformation for peace and security.

Manuals and gender training for peacekeepers

The resolutions and ensuing debates emphasized changes in the views and behaviour of military, police, and civilian peacekeeping forces. For this purpose, the UN peace mission personnel, OSCE staff, the EU forces, and several national military personnel now undergo gender training. These training courses are of different lengths (from one hour to several days) and depths, but most address issues of 'gender', women's human rights, crisis and conflict management, anti-trafficking, sexual exploitation and the abuse of women (SEA[25]), codes of conduct, and the end of impunity of abusive staff. Also part of some courses is the message that women are to be seen as actors, and discussions of ways to include local women in food distribution, conflict settlement, and electoral processes. UNSCR 1325 and 1820 are used as starting points and international frames of reference. All these exercises focus on information, 'awareness', and norms of gender equality in contrast to gender stereotypes and discrimination, some using role playing to address behaviour (Lyytikäinen 2007).

The website www.genderandpeacekeeping.org (2002) offers an e-learning course that covers the topics with exercises and background papers. The course, which contains well elaborated modules for instructors and participants, covers topics like gender and culture, the importance of gender matters, the context of peace support operations, human rights and international humanitarian law, and gender in the conflict and post-conflict phases. Remarkably, gender stereotypes and the problems of intersectionality between gender and other social divisions like ethnicity, caste, and class are discussed as well.[26]

While the OECD DAC *Handbook on Security Sector Reform* (SSR) of 2007 is surprisingly silent about gender issues, a new chapter in a separate publication was recently added (OECD 2009). This chapter addresses gender awareness and gender equality. It provides a set of instruments for gender-sensitive SSR assessment, a list of entry points for legal reform, recruitment and training, collaboration with women's organizations, and oversight of accountability. It also addresses a panoply of reforms in the areas of defence, intelligence, police, justice, prison, private military and security reform, as well as reform in border management.[27]

The hoped for result of gender training's focus on reforming the mindsets of male personnel is an expected change in their behaviour in accordance with the new norms of self-control, sexual restraint, and solidarity between women and men. The call for women into the armed forces is at once a manifestation of the liberal right to enter all professions, though in the context of the protection of women in situations of armed conflict it also has the subscript that women's presence would help to domesticate male soldiers and guard their self-discipline.

Advocacy

Although UNSCR 1325 is an appeal to governments to respect women's human rights in situations of armed conflict, women and feminist NGOs use the resolution to assess a government's performance and as an instrument of advocacy. Women in non-governmental groups and organizations use the resolution to legitimize their demands for the inclusion of more women in political decision-making structures, for the drafting of laws against domestic violence and the provision of shelters, and for the reconciliation of formerly warring groups. The example from BiH illustrates this. In 2007 the feminist organization *Zene Zenama* published a report on the implementation of UNSCR 1325 (Lynne 2007). One of its critiques is that 'governmental institutions, international organisations and UN missions in BiH still do not pay enough attention to the UNSCR 1325; and hence a gender perspective is lacking within their structures' (Lynne 2007: 5). The report states that women's groups use the resolution for advocacy and networking, though their work seems to be rather unrecognized. According to the report, the 'realisation of women's human rights in BiH remains extremely difficult. (...) A combination of patriarchal tradition, social and economic poverty, war-related trauma and nationalistic politics work against many women and youth being able to enjoy even basic human rights' (Lynne 2007: 5).

One outcome of the lobbying by Bosnian women's groups, many of them supported by international donors, was the creation of the National Gender Agency. This agency has formulated a special Gender Action Plan (2008) that follows the 12 areas of concern of the Beijing Plan for Action. One chapter regarding women in politics refers to UNSCR 1325. Furthermore, in 2009 the Gender Agency started preparations on an Action Plan for the implementation of UNSCR 1325 and 1820.

In the aftermath of the war in BiH, the Belgrade located feminist group Women in Black created solidarity networks with citizens in BiH. Contrary to the victim image that pervades UNSCR 1325 and 1820, the feminist group Women in Black Belgrade, a 'feminist anti-militarist peace organization', claims the role of 'responsible citizens', which embraces the responsibility for 'what was done in our name' (Zajovic 2007: 86; also Hunt 2004). With this interpretation of responsibility, the Women in Black organization attends the Srebrenica Memorial Day and meets the mourning relatives. 'The more we assume the role of the victim, the less responsible and active we are as citizens – and vice versa. Assuming responsibility is in itself an act of resistance to patriarchy. It is an empowering process of gaining autonomy'. Resistance to patriarchy in its manifestation of war, sexism, nationalism, and militarism would diminish control over women and encourage them 'to recognize their own power' (ibid.). Occasionally, the group refers to UNSCR 1325 in their publications and street actions.[28]

The group denounces the patriarchal interpretation of women's care for the nation conceptualized in the 'woman as actor' role of UNSCR 1325 and 1820, rejecting imposed identities, and drafting a feminist ethic of care. This feminist ethic of care conjoins solidarity and peace, moral sensitivity, emotional protection, and empathy with suffering. 'By taking care of victims of crimes committed in my name, I get rid of the burden of guilt and anxiety created by the suffering inflicted on others' (ibid.: 89). Furthermore, this ethic also means 'serving justice and creating ties (…) in extra-judicial relationships' (ibid.: 90). In addition, though it welcomes the actions of the International Criminal Tribunal for Former Yugoslavia in The Hague, the group promotes an alternative legal system that identifies criminal accountability for those complicit in war, including journalists, the Serb Orthodox Church, and the Serbian Academy of Arts and Science, who all spread nationalist, warmongering messages.

New methods of transitional justice like women's popular tribunals, the monitoring of trials of war criminals, the remembrance of atrocities, as well as of anti-war protest, the renaming of streets and public places, theatre performances, photo and art exhibitions and films about war protests, and the collecting of testimonies from those affected by war should keep the feeling of moral responsibility alive (ibid.: 96 ff). For example, mourning women at the Srebrenica memorial site hold posters that portray the 'Bosnian girl' with the ethno-misogynist lines from the walls of the Dutchbat camp.[29] The appropriation of this symbolic violence, first by an artist and then by those who were the target of this violence is a protest against and an accusation of all who tolerated it. Publications and recordings on homepages on the Internet are a general strategy to keep these war memories from being forgotten. Only occasionally do the publications refer to UNSCR 1325[30], the creativity and strength of the group seeming to come from its own activism.

In Liberia the dynamics are different from BiH. Whereas in 1995, the time of the peace settlement in BiH, the UNSCR on women, peace, and security did not yet exist, and the Dayton agreement was on the governmental level, in 2003 the peace talks for Liberia could use UNSCR 1325. The Liberian women's organizations at the Accra peace talks on Liberia held a strategic planning meeting in August 2003, and issued the so-called Golden Tulip Declaration of Liberian Women. This declaration explicitly referred to UNSCR 1325, demanding the participation of women in all matters of peacebuilding[31] in the ongoing peace process. Thus, WIPNET already had an internationally backed legitimization for its demand that women and women's concerns be included in the peace settlement.

The work of the Truth and Reconciliation Commission of Liberia was also inspired by UNSCR 1325. By the end of 2009, the TRC released its report, which contains a special appendix regarding women and the conflict. It recalls the engagement of the Liberian peace women in 'lobbying and mediating with warring factions and other delegates to advocate for peace and press for its urgency. They then successfully brought the major warring groups together' (TRC 2009: 6). The TRC had established a committee on gender with national and international representatives and a gender unit that collected and processed the statements. A TRC Act was formulated that called for the provision of witness protection for children and women whose telling of their stories may cause them to experience trauma, stigmatization, or threats, and that no fewer than four of the nine commissioners should be women. 'The TRC Act is explicit in its call for the participation and inclusion of women. It reaffirms the commitment of the Liberian people to "international conventions and protocols relating to the rights and protections of women and children"' (TRC 2009: 10).

From the 22,000 statements coded, 47 per cent came from women. Through a strong outreach programme with testimonies broadcast on the radio to motivate others to tell their story, through public hearings, workshops, town hall meetings, and private testimonies of experiences before truth commissions, about 10,000 statements by women could be used. The TRC organized trauma counselling sessions for victims/survivors as well as special workshops for men, with the aim of creating feelings of compassion for raped wives (ibid.: 14 f.). According to the TRC report, at the same time a GBV Interagency Task Force was set up to carry out a range of activities. These included providing survivors with clinical and psychosocial services, their economic empowerment, housing schemes for them and other vulnerable women, safe homes for survivors in all the counties, initiatives promoting behavioural and attitudinal change toward violence against women, and community awareness programmes especially aimed at men and youths. Further suggestions included the provision of economic support to survivors by the government, protection of survivors when perpetrators are released from custody, and an overhaul of the legal system to provide better recourse for women and more stringent punishments to deter perpetrators from committing further violence. They also include sex education in schools to decrease unwanted teenage pregnancies and infection with HIV, the prohibition of the selling of alcohol to children, and the enforcement of the Inheritance Law (ibid.: 22). A rehabilitation centre was foreseen for former women combatants as a way to reintegrate them into society (ibid.: 25), so that Black Diamond and the many other fighters could start a new life and turn to economic activities.

With a strong political leadership committed to UNSCR 1325, the doors were opened to women's groups and engagement in the construction of a peaceful society, free of armed conflict. Unlike in BiH, in Liberia it is not necessary to lobby a male political class for the inclusion of women. Political power and social power are already strongly feminized. Rather, the challenge in Liberia lies in the struggle over ethnic and economic divisions. Whether E. Johnson-Sirleaf's government will be able to create a sustainable social fabric based on equality for all is an open question.

To summarize, grassroots organizations use UNSCR 1325 for a general appraisal of gender equality beyond merely emphasizing security. They expand it into the representation and discrimination of women in all sectors of society, like health, education, employment, as well as in regard to domestic violence. We see feminist groups employing the strategy of using UNSCR 1325 for the identification of governmental and institutional shortcomings in matters of gender equality regarding denial of entitlement to social services and the weak representation of women in government and public institutions. Such activities go beyond the intention of UNSCR 1325 to have women participate in peace negotiations, and claim a public place for women in the spirit of dialogue, respect for the other, and equality for the greater goal of reconstructing society. Feminist methods of transitional justice like those used by Women in Black or the work of the Truth and Reconciliation Commission are powerful instruments for the creation of a new culture of social cohesion, replacing the aggressive nationalism and ethnic identity politics that lay at the basis of war and armed conflict. These methods of resisting war and masculinized violence target society at large and intend to induce the 'cultural change', something for which security sector reform manuals do not have much to offer.

Conclusions

The UNSCR 1325/1820 resolutions and their ensuing appeals portray two images of women. First, they are portrayed as wounded victims of warfare and as the real and fantasized prey of soldiers, often in sexualized or ethnically demeaning stereotypes. And second they are seen as the actor/caregiver with a desexualized, de-classed, de-ethnized, abstract body, who is proposed to be included in male sites of decision-making: the military, peacekeeping troops, at negotiation tables, and government offices. In other words, in hitherto off-limit spaces of male control in the areas of war, security and post-conflict reconstruction.

These gender stereotypes manifest gendered sexual scripts and a gender dualism that ignores difference and diversity in war and peacetime realities. The danger of this gender dualism is that it tends to polarize women and men, ignoring women combatants and male victims, as well as disregarding the multiplicity of simultaneous wartime roles of victim and perpetrator that cannot be grasped by gender alone. It constructs a violent masculinity that needs to be tamed. The Bosnian and Liberian cases show that the stereotype of 'victim = woman, perpetrator = man', is inadequate. Yet the Women in Black in the Balkans, and the Women in Peacebuilding Network in Liberia provide strong indications that women with personal experiences of physical and psychological trauma from war can also have the visionary power to create new forms of solidarity and thought among women from different religions and ethnicities. The Balkan example demonstrates that the proclaimed distance ('not in our name') from the othering of the constructed war ideology can be transformed into a non-nationalist and non-patriarchal ethic of care and responsibility. The Liberian feminist governance experiment reaches out to women throughout the country with the hope that through their empowerment the shattered economy can move towards secure livelihoods, reducing the chance of new outbreaks of violence. The efforts of the Truth and Reconciliation Commission bring to an end the impunity of human rights violators during war while also intending to change the mindset in which women are seen as sexual objects of male dominance.

UNSCR 1325/1820 and its spin-offs in research, conferences, declarations, training manuals, and advocacy target the minds of strategic groups in politics, warfare, and peacekeeping by pleading for a mindset that guides behavioural control and self-restraint in order to desexualize violence. This would also mean that misogynist fantasies and demeaning utterances about women as exemplified in the UN forces barracks in Potocari would no longer be tolerated. Instead, the resolutions made possible new interpretations: whereas SGBV/SEA had long been framed as a violation of women's human rights, recent documents concerning the implementation of UNSCR 1325 and 1820 identify it as a security threat. This frame brings new actors to the fore: the military, the police, and the judiciary as protectors of women. Although men are literally absent from both declarations, they are present as soldiers, perpetrators, and peacekeepers whose awareness and behaviour needs to be changed, changing them into defenders of women's rights. Men and boys who were victims of sexual violence are not mentioned in those resolutions (Russell 2007).

This security frame is meant to create a new governance of war, including a respect for people's, and especially women's, rights to physical safety, thus cleansing war of its most ugly aspects. In addition to a sexually hygienic war, peace should be purified from sexual abuse by peacekeepers as well. A new form of peace governance is propagated, which includes the military, judiciary, development agencies, and women's groups. The participatory ideology for peace settlements portrays a harmonious image of joint interests that should rest on a consensus about the respect of women's rights, now defined as a security concern. Declaring women's rights to be a matter of security rather than a matter of entitlements was a shift in rhetoric that forged alliances outside feminist circles, especially with professional bodies that had hitherto been identified with 'hegemonic masculinity'.

We also observe a hijacking of these resolutions by women's organizations that use the resolutions to legitimize claims to political power and leadership and for economic empowerment. UNSCR 1325 and its successor resolutions are also used to raise funds by addressing donors. The Monrovia conference, the Angie Brooks Centre, the activities of the Regional Women's Lobby in the Balkans, the drafting of National Action Plans, attendance at conferences and courses all depend on the support of development agencies that embrace security concerns as a matter of development.

But, there remains a kind of inability to understand female combatants like Black Diamond's unit. Should their atrocities and war crimes be excused because they are also victims? But shouldn't the male combatant who was recruited into a war troop or joined it voluntarily for lack of an alternative source of income, and who committed atrocities and crimes, also be seen as a victim? Within what parameters is guilt to be judged? The resolutions cannot resolve this dilemma of the blurred line between victim and perpetrator as they rest on stereotypes of female victim and male aggressor. How, furthermore, should we look at the mothers of Srebrenica whose male family members were murdered? The women survived, but aren't they victims as well because their closest social network, the family, was destroyed? This ambiguous status the resolutions also cannot resolve.

We need to be careful to not easily embrace documents that may be an improvement on the previous situation but also perpetuate gender dualism and stereotypes. We need to engage in critical feminist arguments in order to avoid the essentialist trap of female benignity and male malignity. None of the resolutions call for an end to wars and the war economy. On the other hand, the appropriation of UNSCR 1325/1820 by women's and feminist groups to legitimize their actions, solidarity networks, and transitional justice methods shows how a policy document can serve active, self-determined citizens. Despite the critique of and scepticism concerning those UN resolutions, their appropriation by many well intended women world leaders and dedicated women's groups like Women in Black or the Liberian peace women, gives some hope that women decision-makers will use the opportunities provided by the newly opened-up spaces to confront the politicians, the warriors, and the war profiteers with the articulation and realization of human security in all its economic, social, health, and bodily aspects.

Notes

1 The opinions articulated in this paper are my own and not necessarily shared by my employer. My thanks go to Gunther Zimmer for his comments on a draft version of this chapter. I also thank Christine Sylvester for her encouragement to write this chapter and for her directions for the revision of the first draft: last, I express my gratitude to Rob Wessing for his English language editing.
2 Widespread sexual violence was also part of the Indonesian occupation of Eastern Timor after the departure of the colonial power Portugal in 1975. There were numerous reports about Indonesian soldiers enslaving Timorese women, revealing patterns similar to that in Northern Uganda: local women were forced to conduct domestic and sexual labour for the occupier-soldier.
3 Potocari Memorial Center: Preliminary List of Missing Persons from Srebrenica 1995. The Women of Srebrenica claim that 10,000 men and boys are missing, ca. 2,000 more than the official figures.

4 Not all mass graves are known. The total number is estimated to be around 130.
5 http://en.wikipedia.org/wiki/Bosnian_War.
6 See http://commons.wikimedia.org/wiki/File:Srebrenica_massacre_memorial_wall_of_names_2009_2.jpg.
7 This blog contains more pictures, followed by a discussion among some former Dutchbat soldiers and other commentators. The discussion oscillates between disgust, explanations of the situation the soldiers were in, accusations of the world community for its slowness to intervene, and the inability of Dutchbat to halt the massacre. http://srebrenica-genocide.blogspot.com/2008/06/dutch-graffiti-in-srebrenica-sickening.html.
8 Those words are attributed to a Dutch soldier as the Dutch did not differentiate between 'Bosnians' and 'Bosniacs' like the Serbs did (G. Zimmer, personal communication).
9 http://www.kontakt.erstegroup.net/report/stories/issue15_Freiheit+kommt+_dt+en/en; http://www.sejlakameric.com/.
10 See http://www.peacewomen.org.
11 http://www.un-instraw.org/support-implementation-processes-of-scr-1325/Research/Implementing-Resolution-1325-in-Liberia.html.
12 See also the film about Black Diamond, *A Woman's War*, BBC, first broadcast on 4 May 2009, http://www.bbc.co.uk/worldservice/documentaries/2009/04/090430_west_african_journeys_three.shtml.
13 The interview with Leymah Gbowee is shown in the film *Praying the Devil Back to Hell*.
14 In 2006 Charles Taylor was extradited to await trial at the Special Court for Sierra Leone in The Hague.
15 The struggle of Liberian women for peace is pictured in the film *Praying the Devil Back to Hell*.
16 http://www.1325australia.org.au/textdocuments/1325annotated.pdf.
17 http://www.peacewomen.org/un/UN1325/1325index.html.
18 In January 2010 former EU commissioner Margot Wallström was appointed to this position.
19 Elisabeth Rehn is a former Minister of Equality Affairs and Minister of Defence of Finland who has been a rapporteur for the United Nations in the successor countries of Yugoslavia. Ellen Johnson-Sirleaf from Liberia is a former economist at the World Bank who unsuccessfully ran for president in Liberia in 1997, but stood again and won in 2005.
20 Sherriff (2008): 110; http://www.eplo.org/index.php?id=249.
21 The reason for this limitation is my direct involvement as a speaker at the UNFPA-EC conference representing the then Austrian European presidency, and as an observer at the Liberia colloquium in which I also had some preparatory tasks.
22 The journal *Forced Migration Review* devoted a whole issue to the conference (2007, Nr. 27).
23 *Forced Migration Review* 2007, 27: 80.
24 http://www.realizingrights.org/pdf/Monrovia_Declaration_Mar2009.pdf.
25 The acronym SGBV (sexual and gender based violence) found a companion in SEA (sexual exploitation and abuse).
26 http://www.genderandpeacekeeping.org/menu-e.asp.
27 http://www.oecd.org/dataoecd/4/52/42168607.pdf.
28 http://www.zeneucrnom.org/index.php?option=com_content&task=view&lang=en&id=542.
29 http://srebrenica-genocide.blogspot.com/2007/06/milorad-trbic-srebrenica-protests-dutch.html.
30 http://peacewomen.org/resources/Liberia/GoldenTulip.html.
31 Ibid.

References

Allen, B. (1996) *Rape Warfare: The Hidden Genocide in Bosnia-Herzegovina and Croatia*. Minneapolis, MN: University of Minnesota Press.

Amnesty International (2008) Liberia: A flawed post-war process discriminates against women and girls. Available at http://www.amnesty.org/en/library/info/AFR34/004/2008/en.

Bardue, G. (2004) 'We were forced to fight.' Female ex-combatants explain. Available at http://allafrica.com/stories/200402250453.html.

BBC (2003) Liberia's women killers, 26 August. Available at http://news.bbc.co.uk/2/hi/africa/3181529.stm.

Carroll, R. (2003) Everyone's afraid of her, *The Guardian*, 25 August. Available at http://www.guardian.co.uk/world/2003/aug/25/gender.uk.

Cravero, K. (2008) Address to the Women's Foreign Policy Group: The critical role played by women in rebuilding society after crises. Available at http://www.undp.org/cpr/whats_new/speeches/KC_GenderCrisis08.shtml.

Crossette, B. (2008) UN rape declaration falls short, *The Nation*, 14 July. Available at http://www.thenation.com/article/un-rape-declaration-falls-short.

Council of the European Union (2008) Comprehensive approach to the EU implementation of the United Nations Security Council Resolutions 1325 and 1820 on women, peace and security, 15671/1/08, Brussels, 1 December. Available at http://www.consilium.europa.eu/ueDocs/cms_Data/docs/hr/news187.pdf.

Durnford, L. (2005) Bridges of bone and blood: Identifying victims in Bosnia, 11 July. Available at http://static.rnw.nl/migratie/www.radionetherlands.nl/features/science/050711rf-redirected.

Golden Tulip Declaration of Liberian Women (2003) Peace talks in Accra, Ghana, 15 March. Available at http://www.peacewomen.org/resources/Liberia/GoldenTulip.html.

Hunt, S. (2004) *This Was Not Our War. Bosnian Women Reclaiming the Peace*. Durham and London: Duke University Press.

ICRC (International Committee of the Red Cross) (2008) *Women and War*. ICRC: Geneva.

'In their own words' (2007) *Forced Migration Review* (27): 47.

Lynch, C. (2005) U.N. faces more accusations of sexual misconduct, *The Washington Post*, 13 March, page A22. Available at http://www.washingtonpost.com/wp-dyn/articles/A30286–2005Mar12.html.

Lynne, A. (2007) Final Report. Monitoring and Implementation of UNSCR 1325 Women, Peace and Security. Zene Zenama: Sarajevo, October. Available at http://www.peacewomen.org/resources/1325/1325BiHReport.pdf.

Lyytikäinen, M. (2007) Gender training for peacekeepers: Preliminary overview of United Nations peace support operations, *Gender, Peace and Security Working Paper 4*. INSTRAW: Santo Domingo.

Monrovia Declaration (2009) A Call to Action on Women's Empowerment, Leadership Development, International Peace and Security. Available at http://www.realizingrights.org/pdf/Monrovia_Declaration_Mar2009.pdf.

Nuhanovic, H. (2007) *Under the UN Flag. The International Community and the Srebrenica Genocide*. DES: Sarajevo.

OECD (2009) *DAC Handbook on Security Sector Reform, Section 9: Integrating Gender Awareness and Equality*, Paris. Available at http://www.oecd.org/dataoecd/4/52/42168607.pdf.

Paye-Layleh, J. (2003) Women demand an end to violence in Liberia, *The Independent*, 21 November.

Peace Women, *The Golden Tulip Declaration of Liberian Women Attending the Peace Talks in Accra, Accra*, Ghana, 15 March 2003, http://www.peacewomen.org/publications_enews_issue.php?id=105.

Rehn, E. and E. Johnson-Sirleaf (2002) *Women, War and Peace: The Independent Experts Assessment on the Impact of Armed Conflict on Women and Women's Role in Peace-building*. UNIFEM: New York.

Russell, W. (2007) Sexual violence against men and boys, *Forced Migration Review* (27): 22–3.

Sherriff, A. with K. Barnes (2008) Enhancing EU response to women and armed conflict with particular reference to development policy, Discussion Paper 84, April. ECDPM: Maastricht.

Specht, I. (2006) *Red Shoes: Experiences of Girl-Combatants in Liberia*. International Labour Office: Geneva. Available at http://www.ilo.org/wcmsp5/groups/public/---ed_emp/---emp_ent/---ifp_crisis/documents/publication/wcms_116435.pdf.

Stiglmayer A. (ed.) (1994), Faber M. (trans.), Enloe C. (Afterword) and R. Gutman (Foreword), *Mass Rape: The War Against Women in Bosnia-Herzegovina*, University of Nebraska Press: Lincoln and London.

Taylor, D. (2006) I wanted to take revenge, *The Guardian*, 7 July. Available at http://www.guardian.co.uk/world/2006/jul/07/westafrica.congo.

Truth and Reconciliation Commission of Liberia (2009) Volume Three, Appendices: Women and the Conflict. Available at https://www.trcofliberia.org/reports/final/volume-three-1_layout-1.pdf.

UNIFEM (2009) *Annual Report 2008–2009*. UNIFEM: New York.

United Nations Commission on Breaches of Geneva Law in Former Yugoslavia (1992). Available at http://www.earlham.edu/~pols/ps17971/terneel/bassiouni.html.

United Nations General Assembly (2005) Fifty-ninth session, Agenda item 77, Comprehensive review of the whole question of peacekeeping operations in all their aspects, Letter dated 24 March 2005 from the Secretary General to the President of the General Assembly. Available at http://www.securitycouncilreport.org/atf/cf/%7B65BFCF9B-6D27–4E9C-8CD3–CF6E4FF96FF9%7D/SE%20A%2059%20710.pdf (opens when copied into a search engine; but when directly clicked on, one is directed to a commercial website).

UNSCR 1325 (2000) Women and peace and security. Available at http://womenpeacesecurity.org/media/pdf-scr1325.pdf.

UNSCR 1820 (2008) Women and peace and security. Available at http://womenpeacesecurity.org/media/pdf-scr1820.pdf.

UNSCR 1889 (2009) Women and peace and security. Available at http://womenpeacesecurity.org/media/pdf-scr1889.pdf .

Windhoek Declaration (2000) Available at http://www.un.org/womenwatch/osagi/wps/windhoek_declaration.pdf.

Woods, E. and L. Veneklasen (2006) Africa: Women are Africa's political hope, 15 March. Available at http://allafrica.com/stories/200603150516.html.

Zajovic, St. (2007) *Transitional Justice. A Feminist Approach*. Women in Black: Belgrade.

Zajovic, St., M. Perkovic and M. Urosevic (eds) (2007) *Women for Peace*. Women in Black: Belgrade.

Zarkov, D. (2007) *The Body of War: Media, Ethnicity, and Gender in the Break-up of Yugoslavia*. Durham and London: Duke University Press.

5 Ruling exceptions

Female soldiers and everyday experiences of civil conflict

Megan MacKenzie

War and political violence are defined as periods of exception. The violent tactics associated with war have been famously characterized by Carl von Clausewitz as politics 'by other means'; furthermore, war is often labelled as a period of unrest and chaos in contrast to 'normal', peaceful politics. In the current international political climate, references to exceptionality are rampant. The war on terror is often framed as an exceptional war, requiring novel tactics.[1] Furthermore, the policies that individual nations have constructed in response to this so-called war – including the Patriot Act and the practice of extraordinary rendition in America and Canada's Anti-Terrorism Act – emphasize the supposed need for exceptional political responses and strategies.

Giorgio Agamben's work on exceptionality in politics and what he calls the state of exception has been extremely popular and frequently applied over the last decade, particularly in scholarship centred on the war on terror.[2] This chapter focuses on Agamben's conception of the state of exception as outlined in *Homo Sacer* (1998). Rens Van Munster points out that Agamben's *Homo Sacer* is 'driven by an ethical drive to lay bare the juridico-political mechanisms of power that make it possible to commit acts of violence that do not count as crime'.[3] As will be elaborated later in this chapter, Agamben finds answers to this dilemma of crime without retribution in his understanding of the state of exception.

Agamben explains the state of exception as the process by which the sovereign suspends law, thereby creating both a category of people and a space that are beyond the protections of the state. It is a 'primitive' space of chaos where laws can be ignored and individuals can be killed without penalty. In doing so, Agamben argues that the sovereign recreates the very 'state of nature' which initially gave meaning to the sovereign and to politics.

Like many investigators of war, Agamben is interested in understanding the conditions that make exceptional violence possible, yet, by discounting gender, he misses the everyday, private types of violence systemic to society as well as the centrality of gender and the gendered subject to understandings of normal and chaos. Agamben's analysis is representative of wider thinking about exceptionality in its discounting of gender. In particular, analyses of war and political violence all too often ignore the implicit, deeply embedded gender structures that give meaning to ideas about everyday politics and exceptional politics.

Agamben's thought also mirrors the tendency of researchers and policy-makers to focus on the public, legal, and formal behaviours of the state and its agents during war. This type of approach ignores decades of feminist scholars who have argued 'the personal is political'. Feminists contend that patriarchal societies are shaped by implicit norms, behaviours, and structures as well as explicit laws. Warfare is a time where gendered identities are crystallized and hyper-masculine behaviours and identities are privileged and given priority. As a result, there is an even greater need to pay attention to 'the private' sphere and the construction of identity and normality during this period.

In this chapter I focus on warfare politics and the construction of female soldiers in order to critique both Agamben's conception of state of exception and the tendency within mainstream literature more broadly to ignore the significance of gender constructions to war myths. Specifically, I use the concept of 'exception' to examine what I see as one of the central characters in myths about war, the soldier. I argue that the myths of warfare – or the stories that are routinely told about war – depend on a particular construction of the peaceful, private sphere. Women and girls – as victims – are central characters in these myths. Without the nurturing, innocent and weak female victims, warfare loses part of its meaning and allure.

Numerous feminist scholars have accounted for the types of militarized masculinities associated with soldiers.[4] Due to gender stereotypes, men are more readily associated with the characteristics that are valued in warfare and in soldiering activities, including rationality, bravery, and strength. In contrast, as a result of gendered assumptions – particularly those associated with motherhood – women are often characterized as 'naturally' peaceful, nurturing, weak, and cooperative. In turn, women are perceived as the most vulnerable during war and the most in need of protection. Rather than aiming to reproduce this argument, I take it as the starting point from which to think about the ways that female soldiers disrupt soldier myths.

Focusing on Sierra Leone, I show how women and girl soldiers were constructed and reconstructed as exceptions. Similar to females who participate in conflicts in other countries, female soldiers in Sierra Leone were perceived as unique and unexpected features of war. This begs three questions:

1   What can female soldiers, understood as exceptions, tell us about the 'rule' – or what is seen to be predictable and standard behaviour – during war?
2   What can the resistance to information about women and girls as active, strong, and violent participants of conflict tell us about the acceptability of male-dominated violence in Sierra Leone and in international politics more broadly?
3   How does taking individual experiences seriously complicate war myths, particularly the warrior/victim myth?[5]

Women and girl soldiers' experiences and contributions to the civil conflict in Sierra Leone were oversimplified by international organizations, the media, and mainstream academic literature. When reading accounts of the war it appears as if there is one cohesive 'female' experience. This is particularly perplexing because war is presented as an exceptional period, yet there remains an assumption that men and women have standardized experiences of war. It is widely acknowledged that the civil war in Sierra Leone was one of the most brutal of that decade.[6] It was characterized by an extensive amputation campaign and mass sexual violence. In addition, rebel groups were famous for their ruthlessness, their drug use, and their unusually brutal fighting tactics. Despite the perception of Sierra Leone's conflict as 'exceptional', men's and boy's experiences are rarely singled out as unusual or atypical. Rather, it is primarily women and girl soldiers – whose experiences did not match that of a peaceful victim – that tend to be characterized as extraordinary.

Masters has made similar observations about exceptionality and women in the war on terror. Masters points out that women are integral to the myth of the war on terror – but only as victims. She argues that women's participation and resistance to the so-called war on terror is 'written over' with images of uneducated and oppressed Iraqi and Afghani women.[7] Like Masters, I argue that women are constructed and reconstructed in particular ways absent of, or irrespective of, their individual experiences. In this chapter, I show how female soldiers in Sierra Leone have also been written over and reconstructed through discourses of exceptionality.

Part of 'touching war', or taking seriously the experience of individuals during warfare, must include an engagement with individual narratives. Constructing female soldiers as exceptions has meant that their individual experiences do not count as a legitimate part of the story of the civil war in Sierra Leone. As Veena Das has eloquently stated, 'words, when they lead lives outside the ordinary, become emptied of experience …'[8] If experiences are understood as exceptional then it is presumed that they cannot tell us much about the 'real' or everyday experiences of war.

In this chapter I bring in the individual experiences of female soldiers in Sierra Leone to show that there is no uniform, atypical female experience. I argue that these first-hand accounts must be seen as representative – not of statistical significance, or of *all* women's experiences, but of the variation in how these female soldiers experienced war. By listening to individual stories and accounts of the war, one begins to understand the complexity of experience and the absurdity of attempts to classify and mythologize male and female roles in, and encounters with, war.

Methods and approach

This chapter is primarily concerned with the way that female soldiers in Sierra Leone are represented and constructed. As such, discourse analysis is employed in this investigation. I rely on Laclau and Mouffe's understanding of discourse as a signifier of power relations and hegemonic ideas.[9] Also, I sympathize with the position that Laclau and Mouffe take as to the sources and locations of discourse. They argue that discourse cannot be equated with texts; rather, discourses can take multiple forms, including behaviours, norms, beliefs, and images.

In this chapter, dominant representations of female soldiers in literature, research, and policies is contrasted to individual female soldiers' testimonies of their experiences of war. These testimonies were given during first person interviews I conducted with female soldiers between the ages of 18 and 33 in Sierra Leone.

Most of the questions I asked the women related to the disarmament process in the country; however, I was also able to ask a couple of broader questions about their experience of the war. Specifically, I asked women 'what was your most significant experience during war?' Given the objective of the chapter, I think it is useful to focus on this particular question and the variety and complexity of the answers.

The theme of exception is sewn throughout this chapter. I begin with an overview of Agamben and his understanding of exception. I then draw from feminist scholarship to show the systematic and widespread tendency to depict female soldiers and violent women as exceptions. Next, the case of Sierra Leone is discussed and the voices of individual female soldiers are presented and contrasted to singular, simplified depictions of their roles and experiences. Finally I consider what this case can tell us about the significance of 'touching war', or taking seriously the multiple experiences of all individuals in war.

Agamben and exception

Agamben's starting point is what he sees as the ancient political distinction between *zoe*, the original, 'simple fact of living common to all living beings' and *bios*, the modern and political 'form or way of living proper to an individual or a group'.[10] He argues that in the classic world *zoe*, or the 'natural life' remained separate and distinct from the polis and was defined as the domestic sphere and the location of 'reproductive life'.[11] Agamben's analysis of exception depends on what he sees as the merging of these two spheres. Borrowing from Foucault's notion of biopolitics, Agamben argues 'the entry of *zoe* into the sphere of the polis – the politicization of bare life as such – constitutes the decisive events of modernity and signals a radical transformation of the political-philosophical categories of classic thought'.[12]

Specifically, according to Agamben, bringing *zoe* – or pre-political life – into the polis is a defining moment for sovereign power. As already mentioned, Agamben is interested in determining how states can exhibit exceptional violence in the face of existing laws and political order. Relying heavily on the work of Carl Schmitt, he explains that, through suspending law the sovereign can recreate this original state of nature or, bare life, within the political sphere. This suspension of law creates a so-called state of exception which renders some state subjects outside of the protection of the law. In fact, Agamben notes that

> the state of nature and the state of exception are nothing but two sides of a single topological process in which what was presupposed as external (the state of nature) now reappears, as in a Mobius strip or a Leyden jar, in the inside (as state of exception).[13]

In turn, sovereign power recreates and reproduces the very distinction between *zoe* and *bios* that initially gave meaning to its authority.

According to Schmitt, the paradox of the sovereign is that through its ability to create and suspend law, it can be both inside and outside juridicial order. It is made clear that this suspension of law is central to the establishment and justification of sovereign authority. Schmitt argues 'every general rule demands a regular, everyday frame of life to which it can be factually applied and which is submitted to its regulations. ... Order must be established for juridical order to make sense. A regular situation must be created'.[14] In other words, the creation of order, or the 'rule', relies on the construction and distinction of this order from an exception. Agamben argues that the sovereign does not simply classify what is the rule and what is the exception, 'but instead traces a threshold (the state of exception) between the two, on the basis of which outside and inside, the normal situation and chaos, enter into those complex topological relations that make the validity of the juridical order possible'.[15]

Both Agamben and Schmitt place considerable emphasis on the exception rather than 'the rule'. The exception, they argue, is necessary for defining and sustaining the rule. They focus on the dialectical nature of the rule and its suspension; the way the existence of one depends on the other: 'The exception does not subtract itself from the rule; rather, the rule, suspending itself, gives rise to the exception and, maintaining itself in relation to the exception, first constitutes itself as a rule'.[16] Thus, the rule, or 'normal' politics can be seen to always already depend on its distinction from 'the exception'. Furthermore, the exception is defined by its relation to pre-political life, or the state of nature. The sovereign must constantly construct and reconstruct the exception – the chaotic imaginary of the state of nature – in order to demonstrate and justify its political authority. Put another way, normal politics could not exist without the construction of the pre-political exception. 'Chaos' can then be understood not as a time simply where 'normal' politics is disrupted but when the sovereign loses its ability to clearly construct and distinguish the exception.

The exception, then, becomes an interesting political location. Schmitt admitted, 'the exception is more interesting than the regular case. The latter provides nothing; the exception proves everything. The exception does not only confirm the rule, the rule as such lives off the exception alone'.[17] Clearly the exception here is defined in part through its commonality with ideas of *zoe*, or the state of nature; however, neither Agamben nor Schmitt unpack the ways that gendered language and assumptions give meaning to these ideas. As will be elaborated later, the language of *Homo Sacer* ignores what should be made explicit – that any notion of the state of nature depends on racialized and gendered identities and language. Moreover, the normative privilege that Agamben places with the masculine, ordered, political sphere locates Agamben's thought firmly within modernization discourses – something few of his enthusiasts would be willing to acknowledge.

I identify two central critiques of Agamben relevant for this analysis. First, Agamben employs the concept of biopolitics; however his work is limited due to his fixation on law and explicit forms of governance. As Jef Huysmans has noted, by ignoring the everyday, subtle mechanisms of governance, 'Agamben subscribes to exactly the juridico-discursive concept of power that Foucault has shown to be insufficient for the analysis of modern politics'.[18] In particular, Agamben is curious about how extreme forms of violence can be legitimized by the state, yet his focus on extreme forms and his emphasis on law ignores broader embedded and gendered norms, structures, rules, behaviours, and the forms of everyday violence that make up 'normal politics'.

Foucault encouraged an examination not only of juridical mechanisms of sovereign power but also of the more subtle mechanisms of governance that influence identity and behaviours. Huysmans pointed out that while Schmitt saw sovereign power through the suspension of the law, 'for Foucault the normal state that operates beneath, alongside, or against juridical mechanisms is more important. While the former concentrates on how the norm is suspended, the latter focuses on the production of normality'.[19] Borrowing from Veena Das, it is argued here that the everyday life, the mundane, and the 'private', are all interwoven into state politics in revealing ways. Das encourages researchers to look to these marginal, or seemingly irrelevant sites and moments in order to better understand power politics: 'to study the state we need to shift our gaze from the obvious places in which power is expected to reside to the margins and recesses of everyday life'.[20]

This leads to a second critique of the way Agamben systematically and completely disregards gender.[21] Effectively examining the everyday forms of governance that reproduce identity and politics requires a consideration of gender. Agamben begins his analysis with the assumption that so-called bare life, or the state of nature, has been incorporated and embedded within political life. Drawing on this assumed distinction between the state of nature and normal politics, Agamben argues that moments of exceptional policy and behaviour are at once reminiscent of state of nature and at the same time reminders to citizens of the need for the sovereign authority to preserve social order.

Although he places so much emphasis on state of nature and even acknowledges the way that *zoe* is defined as the domestic and reproductive sphere, he gives no further attention to the relationship of gender to this initial description of 'chaos' and the way that politics, rule, and order have been defined in relation to *zoe*. Somehow throughout his work contrasting the public, legal mechanisms of political life to 'bare life', Agamben continues to operate as if ideas about masculinity and femininity play no part in the construction and reconstruction of these worlds. In doing so he fails to acknowledge how notions of domestic politics, pre-political, and 'normal' depend on gendered identities and stereotypes. In turn, Agamben is ignoring how the sovereign and politics privilege masculinity and are defined and given authority according to their opposition to the feminized private and pre-political sphere.

The very notion of state of exception implies that the suspension of law and the internal distinction between bare life and political life is unusual and unexpected; however, a closer look at the ways in which gendered ideas about normality routinely and systematically inform and give meaning to politics challenges this idea of exceptionality. In fact, even Agamben admits that the suspension of law, or the state of exception, has been quite common – or not so exceptional – throughout political history. Leland de la Durantaye points out that through examples from ancient Rome to the French revolution to Abraham Lincoln's treason policies to George W. Bush's policies of torture and extraordinary rendition, we can see that what is called the state of exception has in fact been systematic and commonplace.[22]

Depictions of the state of exception as atypical disregard the consistent, predictable ways that exception is defined. Political turmoil, or 'noteworthy politics', is always already constructed in opposition to the insignificance of pre-political gendered, domestic, peaceful order.[23] As a result, justification for political violence is often voiced in terms of the protection, preservation, or reconstruction of this gendered order. Similarly, depictions of the political and warranted violence during the state of exception, including during warfare, obscure the private and domestic forms of violence that permeate everyday lives. As Kleinman, Das and Lock contend that an understanding of extreme violence requires examining the 'routinization and domestication of the experiences of violence'.[24]

Warfare is an example of what Agamben might deem the state of exception. It is described as a time where 'normal' politics are suspended and existing legal frameworks are either challenged or ignored. The construction of warfare as an exceptional time depends on caricatures of 'protectors' and 'innocent civilians'. I argue that warfare is a perfect opportunity to lay bare the ways extraordinary moments in politics, such as warfare, depend on the construction and reconstruction of feminized normality. Violence is understood to be *exceptional* in contrast to normal and peaceful order; furthermore, violence is justified according to its ability to preserve or restore this order. Rather than the state of exception being a time in which the lines between normal and exceptional, enemy and friend are blurred, it is a time in which these dichotomies crystallize and are held to the light.

Female soldiers challenge deeply embedded assumptions about who does what – *normally* – during war. Female soldiers in Sierra Leone, like female soldiers in many conflicts around the world, are viewed as the exception. I argue that this understanding of female soldiers as exceptions can tell us a lot about the centrality of women to how 'normal' politics is conceived. Furthermore, it reveals a great deal about who can legitimately exhibit exceptional political power during warfare. In the following section I unpack the warrior/victim myth and highlight the experience of female soldiers in Sierra Leone as a case study.

Exceptional female soldiers

Feminists have aptly pointed out that women's experiences of, and participation in, war is wrought with gender stereotypes. Studies showing women's aversion to risk, over-representation in civilian casualty numbers, and their propensity to be victims of sexual violence – along with research on motherhood – are among the information used to argue that women are naturally more peaceful than men and that women are primarily victims in war.[25] These conclusions have formed into established stereotypes and are part of the mythology of war. As a result, women who take up arms become seen as exceptional. In effect, the study of women who commit violence can sometimes be seen as the study of exceptions rather than the disruption of traditional gendered norms and typologies associated with sex roles and war. The myth of women as peaceful and/or victims also distances women away from warfare politics. Their primary roles and activities are depicted as part of everyday 'normal' politics; women emerge onto the scene of war only as victims or as peacemakers.

Myths about women's participation in war are racialized as well as gendered. For example, despite evidence that women have been, and are, participating as combatants in conflicts across the globe, most of the emerging literature that acknowledges women's participation in warfare focuses on Western nations. Furthermore, there is a striking difference between the way female combatants in the global North and South are talked about. For example, research on women in the Canadian and Israeli forces presents female combatants as a positive sign of shifting gender hierarchies.[26] In contrast, women's participation in militaries in the South is often framed as a problem rather than a sign of gender equality. For example, women's participation in armed resistance in South Africa has been framed as a 'challenge'[27] and the experience of girls in Mozambique was deemed 'disastrous'.[28]

I have noted in previous work that female soldiers in Sierra Leone participated in all aspects of conflict. Three-quarters of all the women I interviewed acknowledged that they participated in combat duties during the war.[29] Some of the duties these women participated in included 'leading lethal attacks', weapons training and trafficking, killing or amputating opponents, and planning out warfare strategies. Through this earlier work I was trying to show that women participated as combatants – in a sense I was trying to show that they were part of 'the rule'. In fact, this work was perhaps too focused on showing how women were part of 'the rule' of warfare politics rather than on unpacking how notions of rule and exception are constructed and reconstructed.

Looking back on this research, what becomes evident is the diversity of the answers, stories, and testimonies from the women in Sierra Leone. Understanding female soldiers' experiences of war as exceptional assumes that there is some commonality amongst their experiences. Likewise, it implies that there is a common experience for 'regular' soldiers that stands in contrast to female soldiers' experiences. The women I interviewed did not express a uniform 'experience' of war: they neither exclusively fit 'the rule' of masculine warrior, nor could they be classified merely as weak victims. In fact, the complexity of their responses shows the irrelevance both of the warrior/victim binary and of ideas of exceptional and 'normal' experiences in war.

To illustrate this complexity, below I include the answers of 12 women to the question: 'What was your most significant experience during the war?' A social worker who was familiar with the women was present and helped translate the women's answers. None of the women told a single story; rather most of the answers were in the form of a list. The lists are often disjointed and given in half sentences. According to the ethics requirements for the research, I was not able to ask follow-up questions or encourage the women to elaborate on or clarify their answers. Initially I found this frustrating; however, the results are revealing both of the complexity and chaos in the women's memories and priorities and the limitations to structured interviews. I have tried not to alter the order of the responses or provide a great deal of interpretation in order to highlight and preserve the messiness and chaos of the answers. Although there are common themes throughout the answers, there is no cohesive narrative, no single story that can be tidily expressed as 'women's experience'.

Experience as exception/hidden 'rules'

The first woman, Fatima[30], told me that she took part in the civil conflict as an 'anti-government combatant.' She did not know her exact age but looked between 18 and 21. She listed her duties during the war as 'fighting against pro-government forces, looting and burning civilians', and causing 'wanton mayhem, maiming of civilians'. When asked the question about her most significant experience, she gave the following list: 'fighting with pro-government forces, maiming and amputating limbs of civilians, served as a special body unit (SBU) doing spying, bodyguard'. This was an interesting answer because she focused primarily on her roles and duties during the conflict; further, she was very detailed about her contributions and duties.

'Aminatu' was 18 years old at the time of the interview. She reported that she had been recruited as an arms bearer for the Revolutionary United Front (RUF).[31] During the conflict she carried ammunition, cooked and found food, fought and was forced to provide sexual services to other soldiers. Aminatu gave a unique list in response to my question 'What was your most significant experience during the war?': 'critical health, nutrition and sanitation problems, child–family separation, in camp or in bush sexual abuses, untold hunger and starvation, indiscriminate maiming and killing, massive destruction of life and property'.

Her answers include both what might be classified as 'domestic issues' along with descriptions of public violence and insecurity. She notes the public killing and the destruction of property but also emphasizes the personal health implications of the war, including malnutrition and hunger. Her answer is a blend of accounts of her own personal body and health along with references to broader political violence.

'Bintu' was abducted by ECOWAS[32] forces at the age of ten. Following her abduction she cooked for the forces and – in her words – served as a 'sex tool' and a spy. Bintu focused on the way she was treated in her answer. She said, 'we were treated inhumanely, we were the object of public ridicule, experienced fondling, our lives were always at stake, we were always targeted by the warring factions either to be used as spies, cheap and free labour or sex slaves'. Throughout her answer she repeatedly uses 'we'. It is not clear if she means other women in general, or women in her unit or community. She clearly voiced strong opinions on her treatment during the war and the value placed on her contributions during the conflict.

Beatrice was 19 at the time of the interview. She reported that she had been forcefully conscripted but did not specify what group or unit she belonged to. She admitted participating in amputations as well as being forced to give sexual services to combatants. Beatrice listed her most significant experiences as 'participat[ing] in maiming and amputations of innocent civilians, looting and burning of properties, multiple sexual abuses'. In this short answer Beatrice manages to cover a wide range of activities that involved her inflicting violence as well as having violence inflicted upon her. This answer is similar to many of the other women in the way it reveals how female soldiers were often perpetrators and victims at the same time. Female soldiers like Beatrice participated in exceptional, spectacular violence at the same time that private and routine forms of violence were committed upon them.

Saphi was 18 at the time of the interview and had worked for the RUF as a weapons cleaner. In addition to carrying and cleaning weapons, she reported that she 'screen[ed] young soldiers', including women. Saphi gave a scattered and disturbing list in response to my question about her most significant experience. She listed

> lack of support from extended family, friends and community networks, tension in the re-establishment of a normal pattern of daily life, lag of education. We were the vehicle and fuel to the conflict in Sierra Leone as we were grossly misused, abused, and finally rejected by the warring faction and the politicians, saw and took part in the dismembering of our children, fellow women and men.

In this answer, Saphi begins by talking about the challenges to reintegration, mentioning family and community tensions. She then goes on to refer to abuses during the war. It is interesting to note that she mentions both participating and *witnessing* as significant experiences.

Fatima told me that she was conscripted as a 'bush wife' and soldier by the RUF. Her primary duties during the war were cooking, offering sexual services to the men, and fighting. She gave the following answer to the experience question:

> forceful conscription, forced to be a wife and be a fighter, horrible and deplorable conditions in the bushes we were travelling and living in, the summary executions carried out by commanders for no just reason, the forceful drugging and eating of human flesh as a source of empowerment, forceful killing of women to use organs for ritual sacrifice to prepare amulets and human skin parts.

Fatima switches focus from the coerced nature of her activities to sacrificial rituals that occurred during the war.

I must admit that I found Fatima's answer unexpected. Stories of sacrifice, witchcraft, or traditional practices associated with warfare are rarely highlighted in accounts of the war in Sierra Leone. Following this interview I asked several Sierra Leoneans about such activities. They noted that for some groups in the country, these types of rituals were an integral part of warfare. They were deemed essential to protecting forces, enhancing the stamina and strength of fighters, and defending communities. Had I not paid attention to this individual – exceptional – answer, I would not have been alerted to warfare practices that were routine in Sierra Leone, yet largely ignored in mainstream accounts of the war.

I'satta was 16 when she was adopted by the Armed Forces Revolutionary Council (AFRC)[33] and trained in their bush camp on how to shoot a gun. She listed her combat duties as 'killing and maiming pro-government forces and civilians. Looting and burning property, multiple fondlings sexual services'. Her answer to the question of experience was short. She listed: 'hunger and starvation, weapons, drug trafficking and drugging of girls for selfish ambitions'. Again, I'satta's answer is illustrative of the ways these women blended what might be considered 'personal' concerns like hunger with political security matters like weapons, and drug trafficking.

Sia was 18 at the time of the interview and had been abducted by the Sierra Leone Army and the RUF as a 'poison commander'. She explained that her duties included poisoning or injecting war prisoners and rendering sexual services to her commander. She listed her most significant experience as: 'stone hearts and evil, open cannibalism and witchcraft'. Her answer is surprisingly short and almost poetically vague. She also notes the cannibalism and 'mystical' activities of warring factions.

Tonia was 20 when I interviewed her. She told me she voluntarily joined the Kamajors during the conflict. The Kamajors were a civil defence militia or group that were quite organized and powerful during various stages of the war. They initially grew out of the need to protect small areas from rebel activity; however, they were also accused of some of the same human rights abuses as the Sierra Leone military and the rebel forces. As a member of this civil defence group Tonia reported leading lethal attacks and 'screening and killing pro-rebel civilians'. Her response to the question of experience focused on her family and friends and the uncertainty she faced post-conflict: 'loss of family home, familiar surroundings, friends, familiar people etc., uncertainty about the future, loss of opportunities for education'.

As part of the AFRC, Amma admitted to 'burning public premises and burning pro-government forces alive', as well as providing sexual services to other soldiers. She listed 'mental health problems, depression, separation from spouse, unemployment and lack of access to economic opportunities, relationship problems and tensions in the marital relationship' as her most significant experiences of the conflict. Although Amma admitted to killing and participating in active combat duty, her answer to this question focuses on the way war has personally impacted her. She emphasizes the mental state she is in, as well as the impact of war on her relationships with her spouse and her broader community.

From diversity to uniformity

Despite the complexity of women's experiences shown here, female soldiers in Sierra Leone have been constructed in a very uniform way – as exceptions. In particular, much of the literature and information available about female soldiers assumes they were coerced into participating and focuses on their status as victims. Furthermore, there has been a great deal of attention on women's roles as 'sex slaves', cooks, abductees, camp followers and domestic workers, and far less attention to their aggressive roles in combat. This attention to the coercion of women into combat and the more domestic and 'expected' roles of women and girls during war distinguishes them from 'real' soldiers – men with guns. Men remain seen as the main actors who initiate and command warfare; women and girls 'get caught up' in men's conflict or are impacted by it – yet always remain exceptions. The overemphasis of women's domestic roles in war reconstructs gender divisions according to what is considered 'normal' or acceptable behaviour. Vivi Stavrou notes the consequences of this categorization: 'Not labelling the work of non-combatant women soldiers as soldiering, continues the gender discrimination of the division of labour whereby critical work that is essential for survival, is simply considered a natural extension of women's domestic obligations.'[34]

The 'return to normal' post-conflict for women in Sierra Leone was also presented as a uniform process. 'Normal' was conceived by the government, along with international development organizations and agencies in an extremely measured and gendered manner.[35] For the case of women in Sierra Leone, the return to 'normal' post-conflict was very much associated with a return to the family and a return to domestic, private, peaceful life. For example, most international and domestic organizations working on development and reconstruction in Sierra Leone depicted the reintegration process for women and girls as a private, social process, 'that would either happen "naturally", with time, or through sensitization – meaning talking to communities and families about the need to "take women and girls back"'.[36] I argue that this demonstrates that both the state of emergency and the return to normalcy are constructed processes that depend heavily on gendered identities – particularly those associated with the liberal family model – as well as gendered notions of domestic, natural, and pre-political.

To be 'normal' for women and girls often meant hiding or remaining silent about their experience of war. After 11 years of civil conflict, including the mass displacement and loss of life, the sense of 'normalcy' for Sierra Leoneans must have been quite shaky or fluid. Yet policies and practices established in the postwar context made two assumptions: first that women were primarily victims of the conflict; second that women and girls would desire returning to 'appropriate' and 'normal' behaviour and social relationships. The narratives of the women I interviewed complicate these assumptions. They demonstrate that women and girls did not experience the war in a single defined way. In addition, the way in which they describe their participation in violence alongside domestic concerns, emotional challenges, and family obligations reveals that binaries such as domestic politics/warfare politics and exceptional/normal are arbitrary and useless.

Conclusion

Touching war, or paying attention to the individual experiences of individuals during war, is a radically different approach to studying conflict. The stories, insights, feelings, fears, accomplishments, and horrors expressed by individuals give a far more complex picture of warfare than any account which focuses on 'common' experiences, or unified narratives. Even further detached from – dare I say – the 'realities' of warfare are depictions fixated on billiard ball states, foreign policy, and strategic gains.

As we enter the ninth year of the so-called war on terror, it is perhaps even more pertinent to scrutinize the ways that political violence and warfare are constructed as exceptional. Agamben's work is rich and intriguing and it can all too easily be mapped onto the war on terror. It seems to make sense out of George W. Bush's speeches on tactics and Donald Rumsfeld's justifications for US strategies. One can even take Agamben's work on 'camps' as a site of bare life and seamlessly relate them to their literal modern equivalent – Guantanamo Bay. There is a need to re-examine this work – particularly ideas of the state of exception – and resist the temptation to think about warfare politics in terms of rules and exceptions oblivious to the way gender is interwoven throughout these ideas.

Agamben is determined to discover how exceptional violence is possible in the face of legal mechanisms and established order; yet, if he were to take gender seriously the answer should be apparent. The construction of the domestic, peaceful, and private sphere (with innocent and helpless women and girls at the centre) gives meaning to any ideas of exceptional politics and provides the justification, the *raison d'etre*, for exceptional violence. If one sifts through research on war, as well as popularized stories of warfare, the way gender informs notions of 'normal' and 'exception' is strikingly obvious. States of exception are not atypical moments constructed through the suspension of law, rather, they are routine moments whereby political activity is defined and justified in contrast to the peaceful pre-political sphere.

It is only by listening to, and taking seriously, the experiences of individuals during warfare that warfare myths, and unrepresentative notions of exceptional and everyday politics, can be disrupted. The contributions of female soldiers in Sierra Leone help to complicate the mythologies of war which place women as the passive victims caught up in a male-dominated conflict. Furthermore, their answers show that everyday forms of violence such as sexual violence, hunger, and displacement are very much a part of warfare. As such, mundane violence, the domestic, and everyday experiences cannot be cleanly sliced away from spectacular violence, political strategy, and warfare politics.

Notes

1 For example, George W. Bush, in his famous 'Mission Accomplished' speech declared that the mission in Iraq 'was carried out with a combination of precision, speed and boldness the enemy did not expect – and the world had not seen before'. Dana Bash (2003) 'White House Pressed on "Mission Accomplished" Sign', *CNN* (Washington, October 29), available at http://edition.cnn.com/2003/ALLPOLITICS/10/28/mission.accomplished.

2 See Bradley Johnson (2007) 'Currency of a Calling: The American Exception, the American Dream', *Postscripts* 2, no. 1 (May 20), pp.75–89; Cristina Masters (2009) 'Femina Sacra: The 'War on/of Terror', Women and the Feminine', *Security Dialogue* 40, no. 1 (February 1), pp.29–49; Rens Van Munster (2004) 'The War on Terrorism: When the Exception Becomes the Rule', *International Journal for the Semiotics of Law* 17, no. 2, pp.141–153.

3 Giorgio Agamben (1998) *Homo Sacer: Sovereign Power and Bare Life*, 1st ed. (Stanford University Press), p.145.

4 For example, see Cristina Masters (2009); Alison Howell (2006) 'Reconciling Soldiering: Militarized Masculinity and Therapeutic Practices in the Canadian Military'. Paper presented at the annual meeting of the International Studies Association, Town & Country Resort and Convention Center, San Diego, California, USA, March 22, available at http://www.allacademic.com/meta/p100476_index.html; Moon 2005; Whitworth 2004; Enloe 2000.

5 Here warrior/victim could be supplemented with hero/damsel, saviour/saved etc.

6 Michael Wessells and Davidson Jonah (2006) 'Recruitment and Reintegration of Former Youth Soldiers in Sierra Leone: Challenges of Reconciliation and Post-Accord Peace Building', in *Troublemakers or Peacemakers? Youth and Post-Accord Peace Building* (Indiana: Notre Dame Press), pp.27–49.
7 Cristina Masters (2009) 'Femina Sacra: The 'War on/of Terror', Women and the Feminine', *Security Dialogue* 40, no. 1 (February 1), pp.29–49.
8 Veena Das (2007) *Life and Words* (University of California Press), p.6.
9 Ernesto Laclau and Chantal Mouffe (2001) *Hegemony and Socialist Strategy: Towards a Radical Democratic Politics* (London: Verso).
10 Giorgio Agamben (1998) *Homo Sacer: Sovereign Power and Bare Life*, 1st ed. (Stanford University Press), p.1.
11 Ibid. p.2.
12 Ibid. p.4.
13 Ibid. p.37.
14 Ibid. p.16.
15 Ibid. p.19.
16 Ibid. p.17.
17 Ibid. p.16.
18 Jef Huysmans (2008) 'The Jargon of Exception – On Schmitt, Agamben and the Absence of Political Society', *International Political Sociology* 2, no. 2 (6), pp.165–183, p.167.
19 Ibid. p.10.
20 Veena Das (2007) *Life and Words* (University of California Press), pp.163–164.
21 See also Penelope Deutscher (2008) 'The Inversion of Exceptionality: Foucault, Agamben, and "Reproductive Rights"', *South Atlantic Quarterly* 107, no. 1 (January 1), pp.55–70; Christine Sylvester (2006) 'Bare Life as a Development/Postcolonial Problematic', *Geographical Journal* 172, no. 1, pp.66–77; Cristina Masters (2009) 'Femina Sacra: The 'War on/of Terror', Women and the Feminine', *Security Dialogue* 40, no. 1 (February 1), pp.29–49.
22 Leland de la Durantaye (2009) *Giorgio Agamben: A Critical Introduction* (Stanford University Press).
23 Similarly, 'advanced' modern political action is distinguished and prioritized above 'primitive' social and familial relations.
24 Arthur Kleinman, Veena Das, and Margaret Lock (1997) *Social Suffering*, 1st ed. (University of California Press), p.15.
25 See Jodi York (1998) 'The Truth about Women and Peace' in Lois Lorentzen and Jennifer Turpin, *The Women and War Reader* (NYU Press), pp.19–25; Jean Bethke Elshtain (1987) *Women and War* (Chicago: University of Chicago Press); Sara Ruddick (1995) *Maternal Thinking* (Beacon Press).
26 Donna Winslow and Jason Dunn (2002) 'Women in the Canadian Forces: Between Legal and Social Integration', *Current Sociology* 50, no. 5 (September 1), pp.641–667; Sasson-Levy O. (2003) 'Military, Masculinity, and Citizenship: Tensions and Contradictions in the Experience of Blue-Collar Soldiers', *Identities: Global Studies in Power and Culture* 10 (September), pp.319–345.
27 L. Heinecken (2002) 'Affirming Gender Equality: The Challenges Facing the South African Armed Forces', *Current Sociology* 50, no. 5, p.715.
28 H. G. West (2000) 'Girls with Guns: Narrating the Experience of War of Frelimo's Female Detachment', *Anthropological Quarterly* 73, no. 4, pp.180–194.
29 Megan MacKenzie (2009) 'Securitization and Desecuritization: Female Soldiers and the Reconstruction of Women in Post-Conflict Sierra Leone', *Security Studies* 18, no. 2, p.241.
30 To honour the agreement made with the interviewees, each of the women's names have been changed in this chapter.
31 This was the largest and most active rebel group throughout the civil conflict.

32 Economic Community of West African States is a regional group in West Africa committed to stability and economic growth. ECOWAS troops, particularly those from Nigeria, were very involved in the civil conflict in Sierra Leone during the late 1990s.

33 The AFRC were a rebel group that successfully initiated a coup in Sierra Leone. Though they lost power soon after taking power, many of their ranks joined the larger RUF forces.

34 Vivi Stavrou (2005) *Breaking the Silence: Girls Forcibly Involved in the Armed Struggle in Angola.* (Richmond, Virginia, Ottawa: Christian Children's Fund and Canadian International Development Agency).

35 Megan MacKenzie (2009) 'Empowerment Boom or Bust? Assessing Women's Post-Conflict Empowerment Initiatives', *Cambridge Review of International Affairs* 22, no. 2, p.199.

36 Megan MacKenzie (2009) 'Securitization and Desecuritization: Female Soldiers and the Reconstruction of Women in Post-Conflict Sierra Leone', *Security Studies* 18, no. 2, p.257.

6 Experiencing the cold war

Heonik Kwon

The story of the cold war has an unusual narrative structure. Like that of any other war in human history, this story surely begins somewhere and ends somewhere. The beginning of the story is still being rewritten. The origin of the cold war is an unsettled issue, which continues to engender instructive debate among historians. Reflecting on the diverse ways to think about the origins of the cold war means rethinking the political history of the twentieth century and, therefore, considering the changing conditions of the contemporary world in new historical perspectives. However, this openness to historical reasoning and imagining does not extend to the other end of the story. There is a strong consensus in contemporary literature that the end of the cold war is a *fait accompli*, a universally accomplished historical reality. The question of the end has no room for diversity and generates no such positive interpretative controversies as those about the origin. The story of the cold war we tell ourselves today, therefore, has an open-ended beginning and a closed ending.

The term "cold war" refers to the prevailing condition of the world in the second half of the twentieth century, divided into two separate paths of political modernity and economic development. In a narrower sense it means the contest of power and will between the two dominant states, the United States and the Soviet Union, that (according to George Orwell, who coined the term in 1945) set out to rule the world between them under an undeclared state of war, being unable to conquer one another.[1] In a broad definition, however, the global cold war also entails the unequal relations of power among the political communities, which pursued or were driven to pursue a specific path of progress within the binary structure of the global order, and the actions taken by the powerful states to maintain the hierarchy and to police the resistance from the weaker states and communities against the hierarchical order. The former "contest of power" dimension of the cold war has been an explicit and central element in existing cold war historiography; the latter "relation of domination" aspect a relatively marginal, implicit element. The debates about the origins of the cold war contribute to disclosing how complex the great bifurcation in the project of modernity has been for nations and communities. The origin of the cold war is not merely a question of time but also, in significant measure, a moral question – the question of which side of the bipolarized human community was more responsible for bringing about the order and engendering political and military crises. The moral aspect of the question is intertwined with the chronological one and their connectedness is more apparent in places where the bipolar conflict was waged in a violent form.

Imagining the political future of Korea, for example, is inseparable from where to locate the origin of the Korean War. For people who date the origin to 1950, the culpability for the devastating civil war rests unquestionably with the northern communist regime, which launched, with endorsement and support from Mao and Stalin, an all-out surprise offensive against the southern territory in June of that year. For those who trace the war's origin to the earlier years, the blame is shared with the strongly anti-communist southern regime, which instigated a series of border skirmishes and also crushed domestic radical nationalist forces in a ruthless manner from 1947 to 1950. The latter measure provoked the outbreak of armed partisan activities in parts of the southern territory, which were effectively in a state of war from 1948. For those who associate the origin of the Korean War with the end of the Pacific War in 1945, however, the main responsibility for the civil war lies instead with the United States and the Soviet Union, which partitioned and separately occupied the postcolonial nation after the surrender of Japan. These diverse perspectives on the origin of one of the first violent manifestations of the bipolar global order are not merely matters of scholarly debate. The perspectival diversity is deeply ingrained in the society that endured what was at once a civil war and an international war, provoking heated public debate and developing to conflicting political voices and forces. In this context, the origin of the cold war is largely about the origin of the war-induced wounds felt in the society, thereby making the very concept of the "cold" war somewhat contradictory, and claiming a particular version of the origin is simultaneously an act of asserting a particular vision of the nation's future.

In the wider terrain too, the temporal identity of the cold war continues to be revised as to the question of its origin. Conventional knowledge associates the origin of the cold war with the end of World War II and the breakdown of the wartime alliance between the Western powers and the Soviet state. However, a number of scholars have challenged this conventional view. For example, Melvyn Leffler retraces the origin to the period following the Russian revolution of 1917, whereas William Appleman Williams famously argues that the seeds of the cold war were sown much earlier, during the nineteenth-century contest for global supremacy between the established European imperial powers and the newly rising American power.[2] Each of these revisions of the cold war's origin is simultaneously an attempt to reinterpret the meaning of the global conflict in modern history. Leffler's scheme foregrounds the importance of ideology (the antagonistic view to communism as a radically alien way of life incompatible with the market-based liberal world) in the construction of the cold war global order, whereas Williams shows how the perception of the alien ideological other mirrored, for the United States at the turn of the twentieth century, the nation's own ideological self-image defined in terms of the so-called Manifest Destiny – the idea that America confronts, as a sole benevolent and progressive power, the backward and confused world infested with imperialist excess and colonial miseries.[3]

The identification of the origin of the cold war continues to be debated today, and has even been revitalized recently. On the one hand, this is due to the accessibility of previously unavailable archival material held in the formerly Eastern bloc countries, which enables historians to introduce new facts to the early process of cold war construction and thereby to reassess how state actors on one side interpreted (or misinterpreted) the intentions and actions of those on the other side.[4] On the other hand, the origins of the cold war continue to be a vital question in relation to the explicit and implicit historical dimensions and meanings mentioned earlier. There is a notable tendency now in the international history of the cold war to bring the implicit, hierarchical dimension of the global bipolar order to the foreground of this ordering, thus challenging the traditional preeminence of the explicit, East/West reciprocal dimension. In this development, the history of the cold war is increasingly about a particular power structure of domination, invented and realized along the bipolarization of modernity, rather than the contest of power waged between opposing versions and visions of modernity.

While the origin of the cold war remains unsettled to date and is therefore commonly expressed in the plural noun of "origins" in contemporary debate, the same is not true of the opposite end of cold war history. There is no plurality of time–space in our conception of the end of the cold war. In the media and across academic communities, it is widely assumed that the era of the cold war ended when the Berlin Wall fell in November 1989. In the subsequent decade, "after the fall" became the most popular means of expressing what was then perceived to be the new, hopeful spirit of the time and to contextualize contemporaneous events and developments on the basis of a radical rupture in time. The idiom has since become part of the language of social sciences, functioning as an essential spatio-temporal marker in discourses about new empirical realities and new conceptual tools. There have been prolific discussions about a new global order and new social and cultural forms after the cold war, and these include propositions about novel analytical tools in accordance with the changed empirical world. These discourses advanced on the premise that the world "after the fall" would be substantively different from the world before the fall and that the new world required new instruments of description and analysis. Analytical discourses about new instruments of knowledge typically begin with a note about the fall of the Berlin Wall or other similar ways to express the end of the bipolar era, before they set out to chart the specific political, economic, and cultural issues with which the analyses are concerned. This way, "after 1989" or "after the End" works in most contemporary analytical discourse as an indicator of the novelty of knowledge; a sign that the presented discourse is about aspects of the world here and now, and not about the defunct order of things from the closed, non-existent era.

The general consensus about the end of the cold war in chronological terms relates to a broad consent about the moral implications of the great End. The cold war ended because the communist system ran out of steam to compete with the capitalist economy and liberal democracy. The Western industrial powers are not to be blamed for the demise in the communist polities, apart from having succeeded in building a system that is economically more efficient and organizationally superior. The year 1989 is the new "year zero," from which victorious liberal capitalism would herald a powerful move to transcend the ideological history that had entrapped humanity for a century.[5] These opinions of "triumphant liberalism" about the West's bloodless, peaceful victory against the East in the war of ideologies and in the competition between contrary versions of modernity were widely accepted during the first half of the 1990s.[6] Contrary voices and opposing interpretations existed at the time, and these have gained more decisiveness and coherence in subsequent years. Some pointed out the fragmenting, "disorder" aspect of the new world order; others highlighted a fundamental continuity, across the threshold of 1989, in the hegemonic propensity of American power.[7] The end of the cold war generated a multiplicity of ideas about the new order, and the contemporary transition is depicted "as a shift for the better, or for worse," depending on the perspective from which the contemporary history is seen.[8] Nevertheless, the dissenting or pessimistic voices shared with the triumphant or optimistic voices the premise and certainty that the end of the cold war was a given reality. As Ian Clark notes, "Whether inaugurating something better or worse, the end of the Cold War was viewed by both sets of proponents as a significant turning point."[9] On the basis of this tacit consensus across different interpretive communities, the story of the cold war came to take on a singular, universal point of terminus.

The French political scientist Zaki Laïdi argues that in the cold war conflict, power and meaning were two sides of the same coin. Each of the two leading state actors offered a global meaning of the cold war within each geopolitical sphere it dominated.[10] The cold war was as much a "battle for the appropriation of meaning" between two competing teleological systems of historical progress as a battle for power between two competing social systems.[11] Laïdi believes that the appropriation of the meaning of progress was the fundamental origin of the cold war, "the first and only great polarization of modern History."[12] The historian of America's Vietnam War Christian Appy also emphasizes the politics of knowledge in the constitution of the cold war order. According to Appy, the cold war was not only a struggle for power but also a struggle for the meaning of that power struggle; that is, a "struggle for the word" as well as a "struggle for the world."[13] Unlike Laïdi, who considers the philosophy of history as the main battlefield for the appropriation and contest of meaning, Appy's notion of semantic struggle avoids any unitary explanation of the global struggle. Instead, Appy highlights the plurality in the "struggle for the world" and advocates the need to account for the variety of ways in which the struggle was perceived and understood by the different bodies of actors involved in it.[14]

Why then is the "struggle for the word" engaged today in such a selective way as described above? What makes the end of the cold war an inappropriate subject for a semantic struggle? When we say the cold war is over, whose cold war and which dimension of the cold war do we refer to? Does the cold war end the same way everywhere, or did people live through the "struggle for the world" in the same way everywhere?

***

After the end of World War II, many communities in Greece were divided between the supporters of the communist partisan forces and those who supported the government's anti-communist drive.[15] In one village seized by the chaotic civil war, in the country's northeastern region, a partisan supporter was arrested in his home and subsequently sent to a prison camp on a remote island. The arrest was carried out by a group of men from outside the village, including one who was wearing a hood. The villagers later learned that the masked man was the arrested man's brother. Many people left the village after the civil war and now live in distant places. When these people later returned to their homeland for a visit, the remaining villagers organized a welcoming feast. The two brothers joined these gatherings if the visitors happened to be their close relatives or friends. However, the villagers had not heard any greeting or conversation exchanged between these two men during many such occasions in the past decades.

The civil war in Greece (1946–1949) was intimately connected to the civil war in Korea (1950–1953) in the international history of the cold war. They were both an "international civil war," partly driven by the Truman Doctrine of 1947 and also grounded in the polarization of the society into radical nationalist forces and anti-communist nationalist forces.[16] The Truman Doctrine announced the United States' active global leadership in the struggle against international communism, and the two civil wars marked the militarization and globalization of this struggle.[17] Truman in fact referred to Korea as "the Greece of the Far East" when a war broke out in the peninsula and said, "If we are tough enough now, if we stand up to [the communists] like we did in Greece three years ago, they won't take over the whole Middle East."[18] In the southeastern region of the peninsula, there is a village once known as the region's *moskva* (Moscow) – the wartime reference for a communist stronghold.[19] Each year, people originally from this village return to their homeland in order to join the ceremony held on behalf of the family and village ancestors. On these periodic occasions, the relatives from distant places are pleased to meet each other and exchange news – but not always so.

When a man cautiously suggested to his lineage elders recently that the family might consider repairing a neglected ancestral tomb, this broke the harmony of the family meal held after the ancestral rite. One elder left the room in fury and other elders remained silent throughout the ceremonial meal. The man who proposed the idea was the adopted son of the person buried in the neglected tomb, having been selected as such by the family elders for a ritual purpose, and the elder whom he offended happened to be a close relative of the deceased. The ancestor had been a prominent anti-colonial, communist activist before he died at a young age without a male descendent; the elder's children were among the several dozen village youths who left the village together with the retreating communist army in the chaos of the civil war. The elder believes that this catastrophe in village history and family continuity could have been avoided if the ancestor buried in the neglected tomb had not brought the seeds of "red ideology" to the village in the first place. Beautifying the ancestral tomb was unacceptable to this elder, who believed that he had lost, because of the ancestor, the social basis on which he could be remembered as a family ancestor after his death.

The morality of ancestor worship is as strong in Vietnamese cultural tradition as in Korean. These two countries also share the common historical experience of being important sites and symbols in Asia for the American leadership in the global struggle against the threat of communism.[20] Since the end of the 1980s, when the Vietnamese political leadership initiated a general economic reform and regulated political liberalization in the country, there has been a strong revival of ancestral rituals in Vietnamese villages. These rituals were previously discouraged by the state hierarchy who regarded them as backward customs incompatible with the modern secular, revolutionary society.[21] A notable aspect of the ritual revival, in southern Vietnam, was the ritual's increasing openness to the identities which had been before excluded from the public space.

In the home of a stonemason south of Danang, the family's ancestral altar displayed two framed pictures of young men. One man wore a military uniform and his name was inscribed on the state-issued death certificate hanging above the family's ancestral altar. The other man, dressed in his high school uniform, had also fought and died in the war, and his death certificate, issued by the former South Vietnamese authority, was carefully hidden in the closet. In 1996, the matron of this family decided to put the two soldiers together. She took down the Hero Death Certificate from the wall and placed it on the newly refurbished ancestral altar. She laid him on the right hand side of the altar, usually reserved for seniors. She had enlarged a small picture of her younger son that she had kept in her bedroom. She invited some friends, her surviving children and their children for a meal. Before the meal, she held a modest ceremony, in which she said she had dreamed many times about moving the schoolboy from her room next to his elder brother. She addressed her grandchildren:

> Uncle Kan admired Uncle Tan. Uncle Tan adored the Little Kan. And the two were sick of the thought that they might meet in a battle. I prayed to the sprits of Marble Mountains that my two boys should never meet. The goddess listened. The boys never met. The goddess carried them away to different directions so that they cannot meet. The gracious goddess carried them too far. She took my prayer and was worried. To be absolutely sure that the boys don't meet in this world, the goddess took them to her world, both of them. We can't blame the goddess. So, here we are. My two children met finally. I won't be around for much longer. You, my children, should look after your uncles. They don't have children, but they have many nephews and nieces. Remember this, my children. Respect your uncles.[22]

These Vietnamese brothers can help each other to overcome the bipolar structure of enmity, even if they are both dead. This imaginative reciprocity has been one of the prominent aspects of the recent ritual revival in the southern regions. The memorabilia of the former "counter-revolutionary" South Vietnamese soldiers and other hitherto socially stigmatized historical identities became increasingly visible in the domestic and communal ritual space. Before the reform, the Vietnamese public ritual space was exclusively for the memory of the fallen revolutionary combatants from the Vietnam–American war. It is now increasingly becoming open to the memories of the dead from both sides of the war and is therefore in conflict with the state-controlled public institution of commemoration, where one sees no records of deaths from what the Vietnamese call *ben kia* ("that side," meaning the American side).

Benedict Anderson writes, "Vietnam and Indonesia came together for me in a new way" through a series of events in the mid-1960s.[23] The two societies were seldom considered in comparative terms by specialists on Southeast Asia before the events of the 1960s, according to Anderson, whereas after these events, their political histories appeared to be connected to each other and to the wider horizon of international politics. A large territory of Indonesia was devastated by the anti-communist terror campaigns waged amidst a political crisis in 1965–1966, resulting in an estimated one million human casualties. The anthropologist Robert Lemelson's remarkable documentary film released in 2009, *40 Years of Silence: An Indonesian Tragedy*, movingly shows how the legacy of extreme political violence from this era continues to haunt Balinese and Javanese lives today.

The film follows several Balinese and their post-1965 lives. One of them is a daughter of an ethnic Chinese family, whose father was involved in radical democratic political movement during the Sukarno era. The brutal death of her father in 1965 led to the social stigmatization and economic hardship of the surviving family after the massacre. In the subsequent era of democratization leading to the fall of Suharto's rule in 1998, the family's daughter turned into a locally prominent human rights activist. She struggled to lay in rest and move beyond the painful memory of the family's past sufferings; her tireless effort included the moving scene of her mobilizing aids and charities for the victims of a recent natural disaster in her old natal homeland. Some of these victims were the perpetrators of the violence in 1965 that killed the woman's father.

The film also features a man who returns to his home village after years of absence since childhood. The village is silently yet bitterly divided in its memory of the chaos of 1965, and the returnee has to face neighbors who were directly responsible for the death of his father and his other close relatives. His attempt to make peace with one of the culpable fails and faces instead bitter disapproval from his surviving relatives; he is also trying to reconcile the memory of his mother, who he long believed had abandoned him. The man learns, slowly and painfully, how his mother's decision to marry one of the killers of her late husband, which forced her to leave her child behind, was her only option to save the child at the time. Another survivor appearing in the film did not leave home after the mass killing of 1965, which he narrowly escaped by hiding on a tree but which he witnessed from the top of the tree. He suffers from having witnessed the extreme violence and has sought help from traditional healers in the hope to be free from the visions and voices that troubled him. While working in the field, he wears the army uniform that he purchased from the marketplace. The field abounds with ghosts, the man believes, and, in his past experience, they did not dare to approach him to cause burning pains in his heart, if he was dressed in the military uniform and combat helmet. The villager believes that the many communist ghosts in the village field are still frightened of the military.

***

These communal developments and conflicts are common in societies where people experienced the cold war in forms other than the "long peace" – the idiom with which the historian John Lewis Gaddis characterizes the international environment in the second half of the twentieth century, partly in contrast to the war torn era of the first half.[24] Gaddis believes that the bipolar structure of the world order, despite the many anomalies and negative effects it generated, contributed to containing an overt armed confrontation among industrial powers. As Walter LaFeber notes, however, this view of the cold war speaks a half truth of bipolar history.[25] The view represents the dominant Western (and also the Soviet) experience of the cold war as an "imaginary war," referring to the politics of competitively preparing for war in the hope of avoiding an actual outbreak of war, whereas identifying the second half of the twentieth century as an exceptionally long period of international peace would be hardly intelligible to most of the rest of the world.[26] The cold war era resulted in forty million human casualties of war in different parts of the world as LaFeber mentions; how to reconcile this exceptionally violent historical reality with the predominant Western perception of an exceptionally long peace is a crucial question for grasping the meaning of the global cold war.[27] According to Bruce Cumings, it is necessary to balance the dominant "balance of power" conception of the cold war, on which the idea of the "long peace" is based, with the reality of the "balance of terror" experienced in the wide world.[28]

The cold war was a global conflict. Yet this does not mean that the conflict was experienced on the same terms all over the world. One way to think about the cold war's encompassing but variable political realities is already being implicated in its name. The cold war is both the general reference for the global bipolar conflict and the representation of this conflict from a particular regional point of view. Societies varyingly endured the political history of the cold war as an imaginary war or as other than imaginary, with or without large-scale violence and human suffering. Cold war politics permeated developed and underdeveloped societies, Western and non-Western states, and colonial powers and colonized nations: it was a truly global reality in this sense. However, the historical experience and the collective memory of the cold war have aspects of radical divergence across regions and across societies. The cold war experienced as a long peace and one as a total war may not be considered within a single framework, unless this framework is formulated in such a way that it may accommodate the experiential contraries and deal with the semantic contradiction embedded in the idea of the cold war.

The political history of the cold war has primarily been the concern of diplomatic history and international relations. In places where the cold war was waged as a civil war or in other forms of radical and violent bifurcation of social forces, however, its history may not be relegated merely to the specialty of these disciplines. In these places, bipolar politics permeated national society, traditional community, family relations, and individual identity. Diplomatic history alone, in such contexts, cannot do justice to the complex, multi-level reality of political confrontation unless it is creatively combined with social history. The bipolar conflict evolved not only according to the intentions of the superpower state actors but also on the basis of existing, locally specific structural and normative conditions and orientations. The popularity of communist partisans in post-World-War-II Greece was related to their moral strength as an active nationalist resistance force against the German and Italian occupations during the war; the same can be said about the Vietnamese and Korean communists with respect to their resistance to the colonial occupations by France and Japan respectively. If the bipolar conflict involved a mass destruction of human lives, its wounds may be vigorously alive in communal existence, even though the superpower contest of power is declared over. In these communities, these historical wounds had been largely invisible in the public space under a self-consciously anti-communist or revolutionary state and they began to be acknowledged only after the cold war as a geopolitical contest was over, and when the structure of power within a political society began to change accordingly. For this particular history of the cold war, waged as the "balance of terror" rather than as the "balance of power," the narrative strategy that focuses primarily on the state and interstate actions is inadequate. We need to develop an alternative mode of narration, one that incorporates but nevertheless does not exclusively privilege the perspective and the agency of the state.

***

In December 1955, the U.S. Gallup Polls ran a survey on the meaning of the cold war, asking Americans "Will you tell me what the term 'COLD WAR' means to you?" The responses to this survey question were diverse and revealing.[29] The "correct" answers were:

> war through talking, not down and out fighting; not a hot war; a subtle war, without arms – a diplomatic war; state of enmity between countries but will not total an all out war; war without actual fighting; political war; battle of words among powers to gain prestige among their nations; like a bloodless war.

They also included:

> doing what you want to do and disregarding the other country's opinion; war of nerves; peaceful enemies; propaganda to agitate the reds against democracy; nations can't agree among themselves – bickering back and forth; uncertainty between foreign countries and this country; battle of wits.

The pollsters classified other responses as incorrect: "little children being parents and going without; too many people feathering their own nest; cold weather; war is cold to everybody – we don't like it." The "incorrect" answers included:

cold war just like a hot war – as in Korea just as many boys being killed – that was supposed to be a cold war; fighting slow – no one knows what they are doing; war where no war is declared; fighting for nothing; real war all over the world; it means my brothers lives as they are in the service; where everybody was at war; like a civil war.

Some of these so-called incorrect responses were actually far from inaccurate, and what was truly wrong about the poll was instead its decision to assign the understanding of the cold war as a "real war all over the world" or a global "civil war" to misunderstanding.

The cold war was a highly unconventional war. There was no clear distinction between war and peace; there was no declaration of war or a ceremonial secession of violence. The cold war was neither a real war nor a genuine peace, and this uncertainty explains why some call it an imaginary war whereas others associate it with an exceptionally long peaceful time in modern history. The cold war was fought mainly with political, economic, ideological, and polemical means; the nations who waged this war kept building arsenals of weapons of mass destruction in the belief that they would never have to use them; the threats of mutually assured total destruction assured one of the longest times of international peace: these strange features that constitute our collective memory of the cold war make it difficult to come to terms with its history according to the conventional antinomy of war and peace. George Orwell's *Nineteen Eighty-Four* expressed this absurdity with the widely cited paradoxical slogan, "War is Peace."[30]

Against this background, Mary Kaldor states:

> The Cold War kept alive the idea of war, while avoiding its reality. [No modern conventional warfare] broke out on European soil. At the same time, many wars took place all over the world, including Europe, in which more people died than in the Second World War. But because these wars did not fit our conception of war, they were discounted.[31]

Kaldor believes that these "irregular, informal wars of the second half of the twentieth century" took place "as a peripheral part of the central conflict," and argues that these "informal wars" are becoming the source of a new, post-cold-war bellicosity.[32] Following Kaldor, it appears that cold war history has a concentric, conceptual organization, consisting of a "formal" history of relative peace in the center and "informal" violence in the peripheries. The cold war was an idea of war in the exemplary center, whereas the reality was one of revolutionary war and chaotic violence in the peripheral terrains: the center experienced the conflict as an imaginary war and actually as a peaceful time; the periphery underwent it as a violent time and as an informal war. The end of the cold war was a peaceful event and opened a constructive development of transnational integration at the center, whereas in the periphery it gave birth to a new age of aggression. In this view of the cold war and what comes after it, it was not only an ambiguous phenomenon, being neither war nor peace, but also a contradictory phenomenon, experienced as an idea of war for some and as a reality of prolific organized violence for others.

The above comment from the eminent historian of modern Europe demonstrates that our collective memory of the cold war is not a modern memory. The idea of modern memory refers to the radical changes in how societies remember their pasts after experiencing the mass slaughter of human lives in World War I and the consequent, generalized, universal bereavement. As such, the idea highlights the breakdown of the center/periphery spatial hierarchy in the traditional mode of representation. Before World War I, public accounts of war time experience were predominantly about the aristocratic heroes and their romantic or stoic attitudes to duty and honor, relegating the experience of ordinary combatants to an invisible margin. The mechanical mass slaughter suffered on the Western Front brought about a chasm between the reality experienced in the trenches and the sentimental heroism that prevailed in war narratives. This chasm triggered a vigorous search for an alternative way to relate the reality of war and to commemorate mass death.[33] Stephen Kern describes this process with reference to the idea of "positive negative space" developed in the theory of art after World War I.

According to Kern, the positive negative space represents a radical departure from the traditional view of art, where positive space refers to the objects that come to the painter's view, and negative space is the background with which the painter locates the central object in his representation. The new art movement at the turn of the twentieth century changed the status of the negative space.[34] In the Cubists' pictorial language in particular, the background became as positive and equally important as the foreground, thereby bringing an end to a long Western artistic tradition that had begun as far back as the fifteenth century. Kern writes about this esthetical revolution:

> One common effect of this transvaluation was a leveling of former distinctions between what was thought to be primary and secondary in the experience of space. It can be seen as a breakdown of absolute distinctions between the plenum of matter and the void of space in physics, between subject and background in painting, between figure and ground in perception, between the sacred and the profane space of religion.[35]

Kern suggests that the esthetics of transvaluation are intimately related to the reality of mass violence and mass death. He quotes Gertrude Stein, who considered World War I and the art of cubism as having the same composition, "of which one corner was as important as another corner": the war departed from the composition of previous wars in which "there was one man in the center surrounded by a lot of other men," and, likewise, the composition of modern art broke down the traditional rule that rendered the negative space an inert void, devoid of esthetic relevance.[36]

In a similar light, I believe that confronting the center/periphery concentric hierarchy in the conception of the cold war is critical to a grounded understanding of the political history of the bipolar era. In the history of the cold war as an imaginary war, the history of man-made mass death existed mainly in the form of disturbing memory and a disturbing possibility; being haunted by the morbid events in Auschwitz and Hiroshima on the one hand and, on the other, overshadowed by the threat of thermonuclear destruction. As Edith Wyschogrod argues, the life-world in the second half of the twentieth century was suspended between the death events of the immediate past and the fear of an apocalyptic end of the life-world in the uncertain future.[37] Beyond the horizon of the imaginary war, however, death events were not a possibility but an actual "unbridled reality," in the words of Gabriel García Márquez, who notes that the continent of Latin America had "not had a moment's rest" from mass death during the so-called cold war.[38]

Delving into the history of mass death in cold-war-era Latin America, including the experience of the Q'eqchi'-Mayan communities in Guatemala, Greg Grandin shows how political terror and routine killings were "emblematic of the power of the Cold War" in this continent.[39] The political history of the cold war is inseparable from the history of atrocious mass death in this context, according to Grendin, and so are the vigorous claims for social justice and related democratic political developments that have risen recently there. Repressive anti-communist politics in Guatemala and elsewhere not only destroyed human lives but also relegated a significant part of the national community to the status of non-citizens; the remembrance of the victims of anti-communist violence and the reconstruction of civil order and the rule of law are interconnected activities. These assertions of civil rights and the revitalization of political life are not unique to Latin America, as shown in the ethnographic vignettes introduced earlier, and their transnational character is partly a manifestation of how, in global terms, the cold war world was in fact a death-world.

Differences exist even within the regions where people experienced the cold war largely as a peaceful time. For the United States, for instance, its experience of the cold war does not collapse to the paradigm of what Kaldor calls "imaginary war" as easily as the dominant European experience.[40] The United States has a memory of mass sacrifice of American lives from the era of the cold war in relation to the Korean and Vietnam Wars. This memory of sacrifice, particularly from the Vietnam War, distinguishes the United States from the rest of the West, whose dominant memory of the cold war is about a painful but largely deathless confrontation between political communities. American memory of mass sacrifice consists principally of the death of armed soldiers, moreover, and it is therefore distinct from the collective memories of death in the cold war in the wider world, which is chiefly about the tragic mass death of ordinary civilians. In the sphere of death commemoration, therefore, we cannot easily say that Europe and America constitute a single community of shared collective memory called the West. Nor can we easily reconcile America's memory of heroic death and sacrifice in the struggle against communism with the memories of mass tragic death in the rest of the world associated with the same struggle. The world does not look back upon the era of the cold war in a single, united perspective; nor can we say, for that matter, that the world is experiencing the ending of the bipolar world in an identical way. How people think about bipolar history is conditioned by how they experienced it, and this in turn shapes what people make of the future.

***

If the global cold war was an imaginary war and, at once, a generalized experience of political terror and mass death, we need to tell its history accordingly, inclusive of the seismic death events experienced by communities, rather than relegating the latter to perfunctory, marginal episodes in an otherwise peaceful, balanced contest of power. The concept of the cold war resists this effort, but we need to avoid allowing this deceptively named struggle for power to continue to deceive us, shielding us from seeing its dead, many of whom are still unaccounted for. The end of the cold war, therefore, signifies much more than an end of a particular political order. It means an ending of the traditional way of representing the order centered on the paradigm of imaginary war, revitalizing the semantic struggle against the dominant meaning of the cold war, and beginning to think of it in an alternative, more modern way, free from the hierarchical composition of center and periphery.

In this effort to recompose the story of the cold war, it is important to recognize that the reality of the global conflict consisted of many locally variant, sometimes mutually contradictory realities. It is important to recognize that in societies that experienced the cold war as a non-imaginary, violent war, the end of the cold war is not an event of the bygone era, but is actually an ongoing social process and human drama. In these societies, the ending of the bipolar era is a long and arduous process that involves creative political imagining and moral practices. The last includes the struggles, arising vigorously in many parts of today's post-cold-war world, to remember and mourn the lives broken by the forces of organized violence unleashed in the second half of the twentieth century in the deceptive name of the cold war. The story of the cold war is not going to find a genuine end, unless we are willing to attend to the histories of these tragic lives and their decomposing remains.

Notes

1 Odd Arne Westad, *The Global Cold War: Third World Interventions and the Making of Our Times* (New York: Cambridge University Press, 2005), 2.
2 Melvyn P. Leffler, *The Specter of Communism: The United States and the Origin of the Cold War, 1917–1953* (New York: Hill and Wang, 1994); William A. Williams, *Empire as a Way of Life* (New York: Oxford University Press, 1980).
3 Ibid., 133–135.
4 Ralph B. Levering *et al.*, eds., *Debating the Origins of the Cold War: American and Russian Perspectives* (Lanham, MD: Rowman and Littlefield, 2002).
5 Francis Fukuyama, *The End of History and the Last Man* (New York: Penguin, 1992).
6 The term "triumphant liberalism" is from John Lewis Gaddis, *The United States and the End of the Cold War: Implications, Reconsiderations, Provocations* (New York: Oxford University Press, 1992), 179–186.
7 Ian Clark, *The Post-Cold War Order: The Spoils of Peace* (New York: Oxford University Press, 2001), 22–28.
8 Ibid., 39.

9 Ibid., 38.

10 Zaki Laïdi, *A World Without Meaning: A Crisis of Meaning in International Politics* (New York: Routledge, 1998), 17.

11 Ibid., 15.

12 Ibid., 25.

13 Christian Appy, ed., *Cold War Constructions: The Political Culture of United States Imperialism, 1945–66* (Amherst: University of Massachusetts Press, 2000), 3.

14 Ibid.

15 See Riki van Boeschoten, "The Impossible Return: Coping with Separation and the Reconstruction of Memory in the Wake of the Civil War," in Mark Mazower, ed., *After the War Was Over: Reconstructing the Family, Nation, and State in Greece, 1943–1960* (Princeton: Princeton University Press, 2000), 127.

16 The term "international civil war" is from André Gerolymatos, *Red Acropolis, Black Terror: The Greek Civil War and the Origins of Soviet–American Rivalry, 1943–1949* (New York: Basic Books, 2004), 187–228.

17 Paul G. Pierpaoli, Jr., *Truman and Korea: The Political Culture of the Early Cold War* (Columbia, Missouri: University of Missouri Press, 1999), 8.

18 André Gerolymatos, *Red Acropolis, Black Terror: The Greek Civil War and the Origins of Soviet–American Rivalry, 1943–1949* (New York: Basic Books, 2004), 231.

19 See Taik-Lim Yun, *Red Village: A History* (in Korean, Seoul: Historical Criticism Press, 2003).

20 Steven H. Lee, *Outposts of Empire: Korea, Vietnam, and the Origins of the Cold War in Asia, 1949–1954* (Liverpool: Liverpool University Press, 1995), 11–16.

21 Shaun K. Malarney, "Return to the Past? The Dynamics of Contemporary and Ritual Transformation," in Hy V. Luong, ed., *Postwar Vietnam: Dynamics of a Transforming Soceity* (New York: Rowman and Littlefield, 2003), 234–242.

22 Cited from Heonik Kwon, *Ghosts of War in Vietnam* (Cambridge: Cambridge University Press, 2008), 60.

23 Benedict Anderson, *Language and Power: Exploring Political Cultures in Indonesia* (Ithaca, NY: Cornell University Press, 1990), 6.

24 John Lewis Gaddis, *The Long Peace: Inquiries into the History of the Cold War* (New York: Oxford University Press, 1987).

25 Walter LaFeber, "An End to Which Cold War?" in Michael J. Hogan, ed., *The End of the Cold War: Its Meaning and Implications* (New York: Cambridge University Press, 1992), 13–14.

26 The term "imaginary war" is from Mary Kaldor, *The Imaginary War: Interpretation of East–West West Conflict in Europe* (Oxford: Blackwell, 1990).

27 Walter LaFeber, "An End to Which Cold War?" in Michael J. Hogan, ed., *The End of the Cold War: Its Meaning and Implications* (New York: Cambridge University Press, 1992), 13.

28 Bruce Cumings, *Parallax Visions: Making Sense of American–East Asian Relations at the End of the Century* (Durham, NC: Duke University Press, 1999), 51.

29 Gallup Polls number 557 (December 6, 1955), available online at http://brain.gallup.com/documents/questionnaire.aspx?STUDY=AIPO0557. See also Kenneth Osgood, *Total Cold War: Eisenhower's Secret Propaganda Battle at Home and Abroad* (Lawrence: University Press of Kansas, 2006), 1–2.

30 Quoted from John Lewis Gaddis, "The Cold War, the Long Peace, and the Future," in Michael J. Hogan, ed., *The End of the Cold War: Its Meaning and Implications* (New York: Cambridge University Press, 1992), 21. See also Mary Kaldor, *New and Old Wars: Organized Violence in a Global Age* (Stanford: Stanford University Press, 2001), 29.

31 Ibid.

32 Ibid., 29–30.

33 Paul Fusell, *The Great War and Modern Memory* (London: Oxford University Press, 1975).
34 Stephan Kern, *The Culture of Time and Space, 1880–1918* (Cambridge, MA: Harvard University Press, 1983), 152–3.
35 Ibid., 153.
36 Ibid., 288.
37 Edith Wyshogrod, *Hegel, Heidegger, and Man-Made Mass Death* (New Haven: Yale University Press, 1985).
38 Greg Grandin, *The Last Colonial Massacre: Latin America in the Cold War* (Chicago: University of Chicago Press, 2004), 170.
39 Ibid., 3
40   Mary Kaldor, *The Imaginary War: Interpretation of East–West West Conflict in Europe* (Oxford: Blackwell, 1990)

7   On the uselessness of new wars theory

Lessons from African conflicts

Stephen Chan

Mary Kaldor's 'new wars' thesis was greeted as a breakthrough – and it was.[1] It met resistance from some for not being radical enough in its analysis, and for not recognising the complex diversity of new wars.[2] Briefly, what Kaldor did was to argue for a new approach towards the wars of today. Existing templates of analysis, established on strategic doctrines and rational purposes and planning, which it was assumed all belligerents would share, were clearly no longer applicable in all cases. Increasingly, wars seemed irrational and their accompanying slaughters gratuitous, amoral and certainly beyond the constraints of any Geneva conventions. Particularly in 'unknown' and 'dark' continents, wars assumed the aspect of savagery, having neither discernible justice in the reasons for conflict, nor just proportion in who was killed and how. The torturing and raping to death, the starving or kidnapping of children – their press-ganging into child militias – were all taken to be something both 'new' and, simultaneously, a throwback to primordial and primitive atrocities. The problem was that the 'new' wars, with their old savageries, were each different from the other. The temptation, when confronted by Kaldor, was to aggregate all new wars together, and the follow-on was to counterpose Western rationality and Augustinian limits and Geneva laws of war as 'civilised' ameliorations of war, against the brutality and unconsidered mindlessness of the 'new'. But a 'new' war in the Democratic Republic of Congo would be, in fact, very different from one in Liberia – even though terrible things occurred in both. The genocide and war in Rwanda would be different to the attacks on Darfur, and they would be different from the wars between Eritrea and Ethiopia. Even if there was such a generalised thing as a 'new' African war, they would be in turn different from, say, 'new' wars in the Balkans, with the cold-blooded slaughter of thousands of men in, for instance, Srebrenica. There was almost universal acceptance, however, that Kaldor had initiated a departure in thought from the way 'old wars' had superimposed themselves – their conceptions, their purposes and their operational requirements – upon new wars that were very different; and, tellingly, which the modern world with its ethical values could neither restrain nor defeat. Acceptance of the new was the prerequisite for dealing with the new and, basically, restoring the 'universal' global values of what was ironically 'old'.

My own difficulties with Kaldor and her followers may be summarised as follows:

1   They are proposing something that is ameliorative, a way of dealing with threat to the existing global order. They do not problematise the global order.
2   They are proposing something normative – on behalf of a global cosmopolitanism, a better version implicitly of what now exists but, without problematising it, the starting point is what exists. Kaldor cites Appiah on cosmopolitanism approvingly – but not his work on *local* cosmopolitanisms which can be very different, though just as complex, meaningful and justified as global ones.[3]
3   They suggest that new wars threaten the global and modern order of states and the way they form a world community. However, almost every new war is fought, not against the conception of the state, but for control of the state or independence for part of a state. They wish to create *new* states.
4   The new wars are not always new. In many cases, such as Afghanistan, they take their place in an old genealogy where every succeeding generation of modern intervention has neglected history and the lessons of the old.[4] These are as much a species of old wars as new ones.
5   The new wars are modern. They may be atrocious – although not necessarily like the Nazi holocaust, the bombings of Dresden and Tokyo, the atomic bombs over Hiroshima and Nagasaki, the Japanese rape of Nanking and, on a smaller scale, the slaughter by US troops of villagers in My Lai and the humiliation and torture of prisoners at Abu Ghraib. Atrocity need be neither new nor old. It may be accomplished by anyone of any era. The point is that the weaponry or mobilising technology of new atrocity tends to be modern. The Rwandan slaughters were mobilised by radio, the attack on the Twin Towers was accomplished by airplanes, alarmist strategists warn of 'weapons of mass destruction' – meaning highly modern weapons – and none of this, along with computerised planning, mobile phone networks and global financial transactions fits easily into the simultaneous imaging of 'fundamentalist' and 'medievalist' hordes.

What I want to do in this short chapter is to depict some of my points of difference with the 'new wars' school that has grown up around Kaldor and, to be fair to her, often reducing her formulations to more simple ones. I want to do this by indicating the lessons of certain examples from Africa. It is easy to make a distinction between the 'new wars' that emanate from the Middle East – perhaps reluctantly but finally ascribing modernity, oppositional values (but values all the same) and a global view to them – and the 'new wars' of Africa that seem simply opaque, meaningless unless explained by recourse to primitivisms, tribalisms, or responses against the exploitative history of modernity in its imperial and colonial forms. In fact, African wars partake pretty fully in the global order and reflect one aspect or other, or many, of the values of the global, modern, nationalist and internationalist world. So I wish to make my point using unfashionable examples from the dustbin of our typologies and distinctions.

The 'old wars' template derives from the cold war where opposing but highly articulate visions of global modernity and norms clashed. Both major sides employed forms of ascertainable rationality and the strategic assumption was that both sought to avoid a lose-lose situation and that stability could be achieved within approaches towards a win-win world order. Benefit and loss could be calculated and put into planning matrices. Benefit was depicted in ideological and normative terms as well as strategic and military ones. When a 'rogue' actor such as China appeared – complete with nuclear arms and growing industrial capacity – the entire effort of Kissinger was to neutralise or channel Chinese global outreach, attach China more firmly to a Western agenda rather than a Soviet one, and thus reassert a two-actor game with its predictabilities and the essential foundation norm of stability. But the detachment of China from the East and its fellow-travelling with the West – albeit inscrutably conducted – meant the Soviet Union also set about its own series of detaching exercises. Both sides began fighting through proxies and, because far away, war in the areas contested by proxy actors could be hot rather than cold. Fred Halliday called this the second cold war.[5] Nowhere was this more vivid, though more misunderstood, than in Southern Africa.

It was, however, when the unexpected happened in a 'necessary' but pariah part of the West – revolution in Portugal in 1974 – and the unexpected knock-on effect of immediate decolonisation in Africa unleashed all manner of competitive and militarised forces, drawing in international militarised support, that the true modernity of war occurred in Africa. The first point here is that it was unexpected. The symmetry of rational expectations for both Europe and Africa was disturbed. The second point is that the Western as well as Soviet responses were modern. In came the tank columns and the warplanes. War in Angola between the new Marxist government and its Cuban allies on the one hand, and South Africa with its dissident Angolan forces on the other, was not a guerrilla or irregular conflict. It was a version of World War II, with tank columns thrusting upwards from the South, to be met by tanks and anti-tank missiles. It was South African air superiority, overcome only as late as 1984 by latest-generation MIGs with Soviet pilots and the latest avionics. Defeat meant the beginning of the endgame for apartheid in South Africa and the launching of a low-intensity guerrilla resistance by the Angolan dissidents. Before then, apart from the colour of the participants, the photographs from the height of the conflict could have been from Europe.[6]

The Angolan conflict might be counterposed with that in Mozambique, where the South Africans did not intervene directly – apart, probably, from assassinating the President in 1986 – and where its proxy forces committed great atrocities and made the first widespread use of child soldiers. These forces were armed, equipped and greatly assisted by South Africa. Their radio communications systems were far better than anything the Marxist government army had. So it was a curious contrast between savagery and modernity. But it could not have been created, exist, or been prosecuted without great modern inputs and much finance. It partook in the global circulation of capital. It was meant to help defend South Africa as a bastion of capitalism. And, when the Zimbabwean army intervened in 1986 against the Mozambican rebels, its first strategic objective was to secure transport routes from landlocked Zimbabwe to the Mozambican coast – so that modern trains could travel to a modern port and Zimbabwean trade with the outside world could be conducted like that of any modern nation.[7]

This much is clear and not highly contestable. The rub in any African/ modernist analysis comes particularly with the wars in Uganda, Rwanda and the Democratic Republic of Congo (DRC). These seemed genocidal (with the seemingly planned and carefully crafted efforts on the part of a Hutu regime to eliminate Tutsis in Rwanda), atrocious (with the use of child soldiers by Joseph Kony's Lord's Resistance Army in Uganda), and protractedly inexplicable (with the succession of factions involving various ethnic groups and various recognised states, their alliances and recombinations, in a Democratic Republic of Congo that seems beyond government, let alone rational government). I do not want to speak too much on Rwanda. It has been contentiously written and over-written with competing narratives.[8] The point of view from inside the current Rwandan military is part of a modernist vision that partakes in global values – although, on both main sides of the early conflict, this was not always so. However, Rwanda is pivotal to how we view Uganda and the DRC. A very small country has its own regional outreach, footprint, ambitions and power-base. It also has its own factions and its own internationalism. There is nothing easy about Rwanda, and the old diptych – Hutu against Tutsi – simplistically beloved by the West is deeply complex under its surface.

Part of this outreach/overspill allows our story to begin in Uganda. The times of Idi Amin seem those of oafish stupidity – although as the film, *The Last King of Scotland*, revealed to a wide audience, Amin was more complex than mere volatility and brutality allow.[9] After his overthrow, a gerrymandered election allowed the brief return of the man Amin had overthrown, Milton Obote. But Obote was himself driven from power by military force that had 'magical' ingredients in both its animation and survival under its first great challenge. At the beginning of 1986, Yoweri Museveni – still now president – took Kampala at the head of an army of child soldiers whose parents had been killed by Amin, rebel adult Ugandans and Rwandan exiles. Many of these exiles had grown up in Uganda, their elders having carried them across the border when they fled earlier tensions and conflicts in Rwanda. As soldiers who would later seize Kigali to end the genocide, they were first blooded in Uganda. Museveni's motley forces had grouped in the north-west of Uganda in the Ruwenzori Mountains – the Mountains of the Moon, as they were named by their Victorian 'discoverers' – and there is magic light and many spirits in those mountains.[10] Although set upon seizing government and redeveloping the nation, and even though he conducted a brilliant military campaign, some of the origins of Museveni were not part of any rational or secular formation.

Almost immediately, Alice Lakwena rose against Museveni. In some depictions, she almost became the modern world's first witch-president – but her composition (for that is what she was) was a menagerie of modern as well as premodern forces. In today's terms, she was hybrid. In her terms, she was host to a number of animating spirits – and it is the imagined provenance of these spirits that is of great interest.

She was accepted by her Acholi people as a messenger of God. She articulated His Holy Spirit, but via her internalised parliament of spirits. Lakwena was himself an Italian military engineer. Ching Po fought at the gates of Beijing during the Boxer uprising. Franco was a Congolese spirit – and there was a host of others. Alice was a cosmopolitanism. The combination promised that Acholi magic would transform inanimate models of weapons and aircraft into the real things. The uprising would be accomplished by the sudden appearance of the instruments of modernity. All the same, incantations and oils would make her soldiers invulnerable to the modern bullets of Museveni. A number of trained soldiers who opposed Museveni, and some part of the rump of Amin's defeated forces joined her. She wrote a war manual for them all, and this included a code of conduct and a health and safety document.[11] After a string of minor victories, her Holy Spirit Movement finally confronted Museveni's army at the gates of Jinja. Having taken Jinja, there was a straight road to Kampala – and Museveni had no reserves; he was throwing everything he had into the fight for Jinja. The decisive battle took place in late 1987, and Alice was defeated. Museveni let her escape and she 'retired' into relative obscurity. But her mantle passed (or was appropriated) by Joseph Kony, who regrouped some of Alice's forces, and recruited or forcibly conscripted more of his own, and formed the Lord's Resistance Army (LRA).

It is Kony and his LRA that have become a byword for brutality and atrocity in today's world. A kidnapper and exploiter of more than 30,000 children, a displacer of some 1.6 million people, a breaker of treaties, someone who has spread his bases into Sudan and the DRC, an indictee for war crimes by the International Criminal Court, he is also a staunch – if idiosyncratic – Christian who fights for a Christian kingdom in Uganda based on the Ten Commandments. Kony abandoned the magical elements of Alice's warfare and based his strategy on modern guerrilla precepts and operational principles.[12] Museveni has never been able to defeat him – partly, at first, because he never really tried; Kony was useful, in official propaganda, as a counterpoint to Museveni and his authoritarian sense of democracy and modern development; more recently because defeating Kony would mean the creation of an emblematic martyr around which future rebellions might swirl; and partly because Kony's expansion into neighbouring countries gives Museveni some leverage in them. It is all statecraft as we understand it – both in its Renaissance Machiavellian and modern forms. And, if ever captured and sent to The Hague, Kony can be relied upon to mount a defence with the full technologies of modern law.

The other figure of enigma, vexation and villainy in the region has, from 2007 to early 2009, been Laurent Nkunda – also wanted for war crimes – and who held down much of the south-west DRC, rather enjoying his abilities to run circles around the 17,000 UN contingent meant to contain him.[13] He did this with no more than 8,000 men and must be considered, both from his record against the UN and earlier operations, a considerable commander. He is the man who straddles Uganda, Rwanda, the Tutsi diaspora and the DRC. He was also a considerable cosmopolitan person, speaking fluent French, English, Swahili and Kinyarwanda. A former psychology student, an ordained Christian minister, a purported admirer of both Ghandi and George W. Bush (with, it must be said, a very French sense therefore of arch and mocking sarcasm), he took up arms to support Laurent Kabila, who became the first president of the DRC; was promoted to Major by the Congolese Rally for Democracy – a coalition of Rwandan, Ugandan, Burundian and other Tutsi forces – while fighting in the DRC; to Colonel in the new integrated army of the DRC; and, in 2004, to General. He then rebelled against Laurent Kabila's successor, Joseph Kabila, and established his headquarters in Kivu, remaining firmly within the DRC. Here, despite denials, he was supported by the Rwandan government, since he both made the area 'safe' for Tutsi residents and drove back exile Hutu militias. He also built infrastructure and institutions of administration and public service. He probably could have taken the major city of Goma, but for huge international pressure on his Rwandan governmental supporters and a huge, clumsy, forlorn but finally effective deployment of UN troops. But he also used child soldiers, displaced up to two million people, and caused great hunger in the region. He did this while affecting Parisian mannerisms from the age of Molière, walking (unnecessarily) with an elegant stick, wearing fashionable glasses and deploying court manners in his interviews with the international media.

He was defeated because he was betrayed. The DRC realised it could not overcome him. But the Rwandan government wanted to use him to sanitise the region from Hutu militias. So the DRC agreed to allow official Rwandan troops to cross over into its territory to engage the Hutu forces directly. Then, together, the armies of Rwanda and DRC captured Nkunda. He had atrociously, if stylishly, served his purpose.

So the hybrid cosmopolitanisms of the actors in the region include modernities in their demeanours and characters. But the conflicts in which they fought take in an arc of countries. Museveni's Uganda was host to an exile Tutsi army that, in the wake of the genocide, marched on Rwanda and took the country. Many of Museveni's own fighters had Tutsi origins. They would have helped him defeat Alice Lakwena, but Lakwena's inheritor, Joseph Kony, continues the atrocious work of rebellion in the north of Uganda. The Tutsi forces by now have occupied not only Rwanda but have become embroiled in the bitter conflicts of the DRC, to where the Hutu militias have also fled. So the Rwandan conflict is fought on DRC soil by soldiers who first fought under or with Ugandan forces who began their own mobilisation in the magic Mountains of the Moon and, shortly afterwards, confronted the Holy Spirit army of Alice Lakwena.

All this seems exotic and surely representative of 'new wars'. They do not seem ascertainable in terms of any global cosmopolitanism. Nor, however, was the European siege of Sarajevo. The similarities between that of Nkunda's siege of Goma have not been remarked. But informal armies battled for both cities, although equipped and to an extent directed by recognised governments and their formal forces. Betrayals and atrocities occurred in both cases and, again in both, UN troops were hopelessly bogged down and unable to keep up with the wars of manoeuvre swirling around them. Both were, by the world's press, characterised as 'ethnic' wars – though, in the European case, everyone knew how reductionist that term was and scholars knew how problematised it should be. *Telos* and rationality were ascribed to the actors,[14] and these existed alongside atrocity. Great intellectuals stormed that Sarajevo was a moral blot on the concept and project of Europe;[15] celebrity intellectuals like Bernard-Henri Levy flew in to pose as if under fire and, in that self-aggrandising manner, extend solidarity; his colleague, Andre Glucksman flew in briefly and declared that the important thing was that the war should be won on television – which drew a stinging rebuke from Susan Sontag, who was visiting long-term and directing Beckett's *Waiting for Godot* in a mixture of Bosnian and Serbian by candlelight and with shellfire roaring in the near distance.[16] No one did that for Goma, no one sided with or against Museveni in such a manner, no one sought to describe a cultural or intellectual project to contextualise Alice Lakwena. These were new wars; they were savage; they were accorded atrocity and not accorded either context or thoughtful grounding. They were primitivisms. They were not even accorded the recognition of sinister rationality – as if Machiavelli could not be appropriated in jungles. Accordingly, we understand everything about Sarajevo. Goma is simply a few television clips of terrified people and inept UN forces driving aimlessly around in white vehicles.

My point is that, in fact, *there are no new wars*. There are unwritten and underthought contexts in the metropolitan mind towards what is now a convenient label. Laurent Nkunda, atrocious, used, betrayed, slightly sinisterly brilliant, now held in a secret Rwandan prison – probably executed without trial by the time this book comes to press – should be a provocation to us all. Not to say 'how terrible' and 'we cannot understand this', but to say 'how terrible' and 'we must try to understand this'. Giving circumscriptive labels we do not intend to understand helps nothing and no one except our sense of categorisation. But then, as Sartre said, once we categorised the world into ourselves and native,[17] we had either to oppress or civilise the latter – perhaps oppress them in order to civilise them – to bring them, finally, into our global cosmopolitanism. We complicate the terms these days, but international relations must take care not to repeat the same simplicities and the same sense of grandeur about what global cosmopolitanism should mean.

There are two aspects to what international relations must do. The first is certainly to seek an understanding of 'new wars' – in exactly the same way as we sought to understand the wars that followed Yugoslavia's fragmentation. The long history of dissident nationalisms, artificial constructs and reconstructs, and recreations, has been written as a series of sensibilities.[18] There is not yet much writing on the sensibilities of African and other 'Third World' wars. But understanding why people fight is only a partial agenda.

The argument is not over what is 'new' or not, but what to *do* with 'new' wars. How do we deal with them? Murithi has proposed a new ethical foundation for peacekeeping and stressed what he sees as the sub-national and ethnic foundation of many such wars.[19] I have already suggested that there is usually more to them than meets the eye – more than simple ethnicities; as much high modernity's fragmented efforts to establish new states and join the international system under different terms and with more intimate voices. There is no project to abolish states in even the most atrocious rebel's mind. But, because violence is often atrocious, a new peacekeeping is certainly in order.

The key second concern for international relations is precisely its ethics. What do we mean by a global cosmopolitanism? On what grounds do we demand or assert one? And in what manner do we propose to spread one – to subsume the world under one? Whose ethics? Whose norms? Whose judgement and execution of those norms? Whose arbitration over who fulfils the conditionalities of those norms? What regime of conditionalities? There are many who would see such an agenda as globalisation by moral stealth. A moral stealth characterised by reruns of old ignorance – not only of others but of their norms; not only of their norms but of different constructions of what is just in war and rebellion.[20] For even Joseph Kony has a sort of 'Christian' code of ethics. It's not necessarily palatable or justifiable, even in the logic of his terms, beyond a very limited extent. But people follow him and fight for him for years. His army is not all child conscripts. In what do they believe? Under which norms do they risk their lives and justify terrorising the lives of others? Until we answer those questions, there will be no understanding within peacekeeping and the advent of 'new wars theory' will be neither a sound analytical tool nor a pathway towards a true cosmopolitanism of equalities in thought and mutual understanding.

Finally, there is a key question of empathetic engagement, 'homesteading' (to use Christine Sylvester's evocative term)[21] or simply the effort to achieve a human linkage of understanding. For the problem of designating something as 'new wars' is its compartmentalisation into a realm of alienated, irrational and usually savage anarchy of deaths and reprisals. The 'new' is then rendered into spectacle – so that, when the television cameras catch up with it, the children are depicted as skeletal victims and women as sexual victims. These images evoke both horror and compassion – but it is compassion towards a condition established by something we do not understand. *How did the 'victim' understand it?* That is a question we do not ask. The sense and privileging of *our* horror and compassion render the persons we call 'victims' as without agency or capacity beyond victimhood. Similarly, when the arch-perpetrators of slaughter are apprehended, we see in the television pictures a beastly figure, almost a beastly archetype. Surely that person can have no self-defence before the International Criminal Court? And, yet, despite the array of legal manoeuvres and publicity stylistics, the 'beast' will articulate a complex set of reasons for his behaviour when finally seated in The Hague. This is not to justify him – simply to add dimension to him, to his 'victims', to all who conduct wars and live through them. Hitler's was a European war among 'civilised' nations, and the Nuremberg tribunal examined his Generals with the full courtesy of recognition that rational thought underlay barbarous behaviour. The minute we ascribe rational foundations – seeking first to discern them – to what may still be savage conflicts, the excluding label 'new' falls away. And sometimes a 'victim' is not a victim. Peace and the end to conflict is not what he or she desires. Sometimes there are conflicts about justice, and people with agency fight for justice. If we do not always discern what is 'just' in what we call 'new' wars, we should not strip away all possibilities that, somewhere in the mix, real people fought for real visions of a just order.

Notes

1 Mary Kaldor, *New and Old Wars: Organized Violence in a Global Era*, Paolo Aalto: Stanford University Press, 2007.
2 Mark Duffield, *Development, Security and Unending War*, Cambridge: Polity, 2007.
3 Kwame Anthony Appiah, *Cosmopolitanism: Ethics in a World of Strangers*, London: Penguin, 2006.
4 See my historical overview in Stephen Chan and Dominic Powell, 'Reform, Insurgency and Counter-Insurgency in Afghanistan', in Paul B. Rich and Richard Stubbs (eds), *The Counter-Insurgent State: Guerrilla Warfare and State Building in the Twentieth Century*, Houndmills: Macmillan, 1997.
5 Fred Halliday, *The Making of the Second Cold War*, London: Verso, 1983.
6 Fred Bridgland, *The War for Africa*, Gibraltar: Ashanti, 1990.
7 See my strategic history of this in Stephen Chan, *Exporting Apartheid: Foreign Policies in Southern Africa 1978–1988*, London: Macmillan, 1990.
8 For three of the best, if sometimes controversial, see Gerard Prunier, *The Rwanda Crisis: History of a Genocide*, London: Hurst, 1998; Mahmood Mamdani, *When Victims Become Killers: Colonialism, Nativism, and the Genocide in Rwanda*, Princeton: Princeton University Press, 2001; Linda Melvern, *Conspiracy to Murder: The Rwanda Genocide*, London: Verso, 2006.
9 Based on the even better book by Giles Foden, *The Last King of Scotland*, London: Vintage, 1999.
10 The Nzururu people who live in the Ruwenzori Mountains regard the area as spirit-laden. Speke and Burton who were the first white men to 'discover' what they called the Mountains of the Moon were overwhelmed by their sense of luminosity. I spent some weeks there in the post-Amin reconstruction efforts and felt certain the mountains radiated a strange energy.
11 Heiki Behrend, *Alice Lakwena and the Holy Spirits: War in Northern Uganda 1986–7*, London: James Currey, 1999.
12 Matthew Green, *The Wizard of the Nile: The Hunt for Africa's Most Wanted*, London: Portobello, 2008.
13 No books in English have yet been written on Nkunda. He has given quite lengthy interviews to NBC and other broadcasters. But see Stewart Andrew Scott, *Laurent Nkunda et la rebellion du Kivu: au Coeur de la guerre congolaise*, Paris: Karthala, 2008.
14 David Campbell, *National Deconstruction: Violence, Identity and Justice in Bosnia*, Minneapolis: University of Minnesota Press, 1998.
15 Alain Finkielkraut, *The Crime of Being Born* (originally in French, this is the only English version I could find), Zagreb: Ceres, 1997.
16 Susan Sontag, *Where the Stress Falls*, London: Jonathan Cape, 2002, pp. 299–322.
17 In his opening lines to his infamous preface to Frantz Fanon's *Wretched of the Earth*, New York: Grove, 1965.
18 Ivo Goldstein, *Croatia: A History*, London: Hurst, 1999.
19 Tim Murithi, *The Ethics of Peacebuilding*, Edinburgh: Edinburgh University Press, 2009.
20 These constitute some of the central themes in Stephen Chan, *The End of Certainty: Towards a New Internationalism*, London: Zed, 2009.
21 Christine Sylvester, *Feminist Theory and International Relations in a Postmodern Era*, Cambridge: Cambridge University Press, 1994.

8   Dilemmas of drawing war

Jill Gibbon

There is a long official tradition of drawing war. Artists are regularly commissioned by government committees, museums and the armed forces to make art from the battlefield, often through the use of drawing. Since 2001 I have attempted to reverse this tradition by drawing the arms trade. This alternative focus was initially accidental, a result of my circumstances on 9/11. It was only later that it became deliberate.

I didn't see the attacks on the world trade centre when they were first broadcast. I was trapped behind police lines outside DSEi, the Defence Systems and Equipment International, one of the world's largest arms fairs. I am a reportage illustrator and I had gone to draw and take part in the protests. Using a tactic called 'penning in', the police confined protestors to a small square of tarmac opposite Excel, the exhibition centre where the fair was being held. With phone signals down, and restricted movement, there was little news from the outside world. It wasn't until the evening, on my way home on the tube, that I saw the harrowing photographs of the twin towers and headlines about war. The commuter sitting next to me questioned the paper's interpretation. The attacks were a brutal act of terrorism, but surely not a war? However, in a formal response to the attacks nine days later, George Bush declared war on terrorism,[1] 'Our war on terror begins with al Qaeda, but it does not end there. It will not end until every terrorist group of global reach has been found, stopped and defeated' (Bush, 2001).

Such an amorphous target raised the prospect of unending conflict. Who could possibly benefit? In the following months, shares in arms companies soared. Perhaps my location that day was not entirely irrelevant.

So, when artists were dispatched to document the wars in Afghanistan and Iraq, I decided to draw the arms trade. This chapter tells the story of the attempt. Because the project has developed largely in opposition to official drawings of war, the chapter begins with a brief history of the genre. Here, I argue that the tradition of sending artists into war zones has an ideological function. The next section explains the relevance of the arms trade as a subject of war art, and the final section describes my attempts to draw it. Running through the chapter is a discussion of meanings of witness, a word that has provided a structuring rationale for official war art and my own drawings of the arms trade.

Official war art

In 1916 the British War Propaganda Bureau dispatched an artist, Muirhead Bone, to draw the Western Front. Needing visual material for propaganda but wary of allowing photographers near the front, drawing seemed to offer an innocuous compromise. The decision represented a significant shift from previous official traditions of war art. Although paintings had previously been commissioned to commemorate significant battles, they were usually made at a geographical and chronological distance from the event. Since then, the artist's presence in the war zone has become the defining feature of official war art. Artists have been commissioned to visit and document all of the recent wars in which British troops have been involved. The Artistic Records Office at the Imperial War Museum now commissions most of this work, however the British army also regularly commissions artists.

Official war art is particularly associated with drawing. In the First and Second World Wars most artists drew on location either in preparation for paintings, or as the final product. In 1982 Linda Kitson drew the Falklands War for the Imperial War Museum, and in 2006 and 2008 the British Army commissioned Arabella Dorman and Xavier Pick to draw in Iraq. Contemporary commissions also include new media; for instance in 2003 Langlands and Bell produced an interactive animation of Osama Bin Laden's abandoned house as part of a commission for the Imperial War Museum. Yet, across this range of commissioning institutions, artists and media, a basic formula remains the same – artists are dispatched to war zones to make art. The rationale is that they should be eyewitnesses of war. This is evident from the title of an exhibition of official war art at the Imperial War Museum in 2006 which was called simply 'Witness' (http://north.iwm.org.uk/server/show/ConWebDoc.985 accessed 10 October 2009).

The emphasis on witnessing in official war art contrasts sharply with the need to keep artists safe, sometimes with ludicrous consequences. The artist, Steve McQueen, was sent to Iraq in 2003 just as the conflict escalated and was virtually confined to army barracks. He said afterwards, 'I knew I'd be embedded with the troops, but I didn't imagine that meant I'd virtually have to stay in bed. It was ridiculous' (McQueen, 2007, in Searle, 2007).

Ironically, he would have seen more of the war on the news had he stayed in the UK. It seems likely that the practice of sending artists into war zones continues, in spite of the inevitable logistical difficulties, because it has an important ideological function.

Official war art initially had an overt propagandist purpose as is clear from the title of the institution that established it – the War Propaganda Bureau. However, according to the Imperial War Museum it subsequently took on a loftier aim. 'Begun in 1916 mainly for propaganda purposes, the scheme eventually aimed much higher' (http://collections.iwm.org.uk/server.php?show=nav.206 accessed 3 October 2009).

In this section I will argue that official war art continues to work as propaganda, though in a more subtle way than when it was first commissioned, largely through the emphasis it places on the war zone, and the claim that it aspires to something 'higher'. While the emphasis on the war zone restricts the content of official war art, the idea that it evokes something 'higher' imbues that content with transcendent value. This argument will require a number of detours to explain the ideas of observation, truth and value that official war art draws on, beginning with a brief etymology of witness, the central organising term for these ideas.

The word 'witness' derives from the Old English 'witan', to know. In the thirteenth century witness was used to describe various types of knowledge including 'inner knowing' or conviction, knowledge based on observation, and a quality of wisdom or a skill. It was used as a verb to describe the act of giving testimony to such knowledge, and as a noun to describe an observer or a piece of testimony or evidence (Lewise, 2000). Although most of these meanings remain in use, they have separated into distinct dominant and marginal strands. Whereas a witness of conviction has become marginal, a witness based on observation has become dominant, particularly as a noun to refer to an observer. It is this meaning of witness that structures official war art.

The gulf between contemporary meanings of witness can perhaps be explained by the rise of empiricism and positivism in the eighteenth and nineteenth centuries. Empiricism advocates methodical observation as a reliable source of knowledge. Positivism, a nineteenth-century school of philosophy, goes further than this, advocating direct experience as the only genuine source of knowledge. In some versions, observation is presented as giving direct access to reality. This idea has been widely criticised in twentieth-century philosophy for ignoring the many ways we interpret what we see, and social influences on meaning (Barbanell and Garrett, 1997; Craig, 1998). Nevertheless, the idea that observation is the only valid source of knowledge continues to have resonance. It runs through official war art.

Although official war art takes many forms, there is one underlying rule. The content must be based on things that the artist has seen. Paul Gough notes that the Artistic Records Committee of the Imperial War Museum 'insists on eye-witness accounts from its commissioned artists' (Gough, 1994).

The importance attached to this rule is evident in the response given to artists who seem to have strayed from it. Peter Howson's painting of a rape in the Bosnian War, *Croatian and Muslim* (1994), was excluded from the permanent collection of the Imperial War Museum because it was based on victims' accounts, rather than anything that Howson had actually seen. And the British press criticised John Keane, the official artist of the Gulf War, because they claimed he could not have seen the content of *Mickey Mouse at the Front* (1991), a painting of Mickey Mouse next to a shopping trolley of weapons (Cork, 1992; Daneff and Stringer, 1992; Gillie, 1992; Thurlbeck, 1992). Instead of engaging in the subtext of the criticisms – the painting's obvious reference to American commercial interests in the Gulf, Keane defended himself by taking the complaints at face value. Having used a camcorder to collect visual references in the Gulf, he was able to show video footage of a toy Mickey Mouse and shopping trolley he had seen in rubble in Kuwait. But although this floored his critics, it perpetuated the assumption that official war art should be restricted to things seen. As Julian Stallabrass points out, the insistence that war artists work as eyewitnesses dramatically restricts the scope of the work:

> The artist who is confined to acting as witness is powerless to reveal those things hidden from the video: high-tech atrocities committed against civilians and conscript troops, soldiers buried alive in their dugouts, the cultivation of starvation and disease by the bombing of sewage and irrigation systems.
>
> (Stallabrass, 2004, p 106)

In addition to restricting its content, the insistence that official war art is based on observation has often been used to guarantee the authenticity of the work. This 1918 review likens the war artist C.R.W. Nevinson to a court witness: 'He is content to appear not as a judge or advocate but simply as an uncorrupted witness. He states without rhetoric what the eye sees' (Flitch, 1918, in Malvern, 2004, p 48).

Reviews of Linda Kitson's Falklands War drawings made similar claims about the objectivity of her work. For instance, a review in the *Westminster and Pimlico News* claimed, 'The artist was totally objective – sketching the soldiers with whom she lived, their highs and lows, with a detached and impersonal eye' (Imperial War Museum, 1982).

The emphasis on direct observation in official war art initially influenced the type of artist and art that was commissioned. The first official war artist, Muirhead Bone, trained as an architect and specialised in observational drawing. All drawing is an interpretation but in observational drawing this is underplayed. Marks are made to represent what is seen rather than to express a feeling or opinion about a subject. The head of the Propaganda Bureau, CFG Masterman, urged Bone to emphasise 'not only the artistic but the realistic side' (Masterman, 1916, in Malvern, 2004, p 38). And Bone stressed that he worked from observation, '(I) only drew what I saw and then only when I had a chance to draw it' (www.iwm.org.uk/server/show/ nav.2341 accessed 6 October 2009).

However, like any other drawing technique, observational drawing is structured by a repertoire of conventions traditionally learned by copying 'old master' artists. Susan Malvern suggests that Bone used techniques from topographical and antiquarian drawing traditions. A drawing entitled *The Battle of the Somme* (1916) could be mistaken for a pastoral landscape. Lines emphasise the topographical contours of an escarpment, ditches and trees, and rules of perspective give the impression that the artist is viewing the scene at a fixed point somewhere outside the landscape. This sense of detachment is reinforced by a small figure in military dress who sits on the escarpment, sitting out looking towards a few smudges of smoke – the only indication of the battle raging in the background (Malvern, 2004, p 24).

Clearly, this is a highly edited account of the war but the manner of drawing suggests objective accuracy. However, as casualties soared observational drawing became inadequate to the task of representing the war. The war clearly involved more than smoke on a distant horizon. Muirhead Bone seemed to acknowledge this when he described his war drawings as 'limited' and 'prosaic' (in Malvern, 2004, p 24).

From 1917 the emphasis in official war art shifted from apparently objective reportage, to art. This is what the Imperial War Musuem meant when it said that the scheme 'eventually aimed much higher'. Painters were commissioned to produce work for exhibition in galleries and, in contrast to his earlier instructions, Masterman stressed artistic freedom. He wrote to the war artist, Eric Kennington, 'I am afraid I cannot give you any directions as to what you should draw – I am quite content that you should go on drawing whatever you think best' (Masterman, 1917, in Malvern, 2004, p 49).

As part of this change of emphasis, expressive approaches were encouraged. Expressive methods derive from a debate running through twentieth-century art about the meaning of realism. Does a 'realistic' representation depict outward surfaces, or 'reveal' unseen political aspects or psychological responses to a situation? In contrast to the emphasis on visual accuracy in observational drawing, expressive techniques use exaggeration, metaphor, idealisation and distortion to highlight artists' subjective interpretations.

John Singer Sargent's painting of a line of soldiers blinded by mustard gas, *Gassed* (1918–1919), is monumental and idealised. C.R.W. Nevinson's painting, *After A Push* (c 1917), is oppressively dark and monotonous. The paint, like the terrain it represents, seems to be composed of mud. Paul Nash's landscapes are similarly distorted and tortured. Drawn with dull coloured pastels on brown paper, *Sunrise: Inverness Copse* (1918), depicts a monotone field of broken trees. Although the title implies optimism, the rays of the sun are faint and horizontal so the sun seems to struggle to rise.

These images were clearly subjective however they continued to be presented as offering truths of war. This is evident in the title of one of the earliest publications of Paul Nash's war art *Strange but True*. An introduction by the Propaganda Bureau began with the warning, 'Some fault will be found with what Lieut. Paul Nash has done here. It will be said that no barbed wire ever twirled on this earth in the forms which are taken by his' (GHQ, in Nevinson *et al.*, 1918, p 87).

This is followed by an assertion of the authenticity of the work, with the assurance that it derived from observation. Indeed the text implies that instead of depicting external surfaces, Nash's work revealed a deeper reality. 'He has got, at his best, to the essence of many things he has seen' (GHQ, in Nevinson *et al.*, 1918, p 85).

In a similar vein, the critic P.G. Konody suggested that Nevinson's war art reached a pinnacle of truth. It was 'the least literal, and for that very reason the most truthful' (Konody, 1917, in Malvern 2004, p 44).

Clearly, the use of expressive techniques allowed artists to convey personal interpretations of the things they saw. However, these reviews claim more than this. They suggest that the artists reveal *essential* truths. Similar claims are made in relation to contemporary war art. This is the foreword to a catalogue of Arabella Dorman's paintings and prints of Basra: 'There is a great tradition of artists capturing the true experience of war and Arabella has certainly done this' (Pringle, in Dorman, 2009, p 1).

These claims require more than a positivist idea of witness. They draw on a romantic idea of art as a source of essential, authentic values. This is a complex idea, deriving from the emergence of romanticism in the nineteenth century, and its impact on meanings of art and aesthetic value. As it is so fundamental to the ideological workings of official war art, it is worth tracing its historical sources.

The term 'romanticism' emerged in the early nineteenth century to describe an emphasis on deep feeling, extreme experience and self-expression. Romanticism developed partly in response to the French revolutions (1789–1815), the industrial revolution and the rise of the bourgeoisie. Terry Eagleton (1990) suggests that as traditional roles fragmented, attention focused on the dynamic potential of individual and collective feeling. An emphasis on feeling was already evident in the term 'aesthetic' that came into use in the eighteenth century. Although in contemporary usage aesthetic refers to qualities of art, in the eighteenth century it had a much more general meaning. The philosophers Alexander Baumgarten and Immanuel Kant used aesthetic to refer to the perception and communication of feeling through the senses (Harris, 2006, p 10, Williams, 1976, p 32). By stressing sensation and feeling as a source of understanding, these discourses represented a significant departure from the emphasis on reason in the Enlightenment.

Terry Eagleton (1990) suggests that the idea of the aesthetic was at once radical and reactionary. In the revolutions of the eighteenth and nineteenth centuries, deep feeling was expressed as an impetus for self-determination and given a collective form. Conversely, however, the aesthetic emphasis on sensuous feeling also underpinned bourgeois ideology, emerging at the same time as the modern state. Whereas a barbarous state maintains its authority through blatant repression, a democracy is held in place by an apparent consensus of 'fellow feeling'. This ideological function of the idea of aesthetic value raised a problem – it demanded that aesthetic feeling was both subjective *and* universal. This contradiction was overcome, to an extent, by a dramatic restriction in the meaning of the term. By the end of the nineteenth century, aesthetic was used almost exclusively in relation to the internal characteristics and qualities of art (Eagleton, 1990; Harris, 2006; Williams, 1976).

This change in the meaning of aesthetic was accompanied by a similar contraction in the meaning of 'art'. Until the seventeenth century, art was used to describe any skill. However, by the nineteenth century the term had specialised to refer to the 'fine arts' – painting, drawing and sculpture. Alongside this change, the romantic emphasis on emotion focused on artists who came to be regarded as specialists in feeling. Raymond Williams (1976) links this change to the emergence of industrial capitalism when art came to represent a refuge from mechanised production. With this development, art was conceived as separate from society, and the term aesthetic came to represent higher qualities associated with art, but not the world. For all that this seemed to set up an enclave of authentic value in opposition to capitalism it also provided a framework to justify the dominant order. The idea of a realm of autonomous value allowed the bourgeoisie to justify its partisan interests as universal (Eagleton, 1990, p 27).

This puts a new perspective on the claim made by the Imperial War Museum that, after an initial function as propaganda, official war art 'aimed much higher'. Official war art literally transforms war into art and, in so doing, links war to supposedly universal values widely associated with art. Far from marking a break from the propagandist function of official war art, the evocation of higher values refines that function. The transformation of war into art is evident in this summary of official war art by *The Times* in 1916. It called for artists

> who have seen with their own eyes, and have brought the emotion of the artist into touch with the grim or noble realities of war ... Then the studies would, in time, become pictures, some of them no doubt, great pictures ... In a word Britain might thus become possessed of worthy memorials of the greatest epoch in the country's history, and a true Renaissance of Art might be brought about under the stress of a noble and all-pervading emotion.
>
> (quoted in Malvern, 2004, p 12)

Here, *The Times* combines the positivist idea that sight gives a direct link to the 'realities of war' with the romantic notion that great art emerges from extreme experience. If artists see war 'with their own eyes', the resulting emotions will apparently trigger a cultural renaissance.

Similar claims are made in reviews of contemporary official war art. In 2004 Langlands and Bell were shortlisted for the Turner Prize for their official art about the Afghanistan war. This is an extract from the Tate catalogue for the exhibition: 'Langlands & Bell present elegant and lasting work in an intelligent, but ultimately impartial, style ... The poignant ambiguity of these works ultimately reflects the stark realities of the aftermath of war' (Tate Britain, 2004, p 9).

The repetition of 'ultimately' and the description of the work as 'lasting' evokes a romantic idea of higher, timeless values, apparently achieved through the artists' contact with the 'stark realities' of war. As in the extract from *The Times*, romantic and positivist discourses frame a contested war in a realm of supposedly universal values.

Accounts of official war art do not only suggest that artists use war to produce great art, they also imply that the experience of war matures an artist's practice. In 1919, Nash described the effect of the war on his development as an artist.

> My war experiences have developed me – certainly on the technical side. I think I have almost discovered my sense of colour which was very weak before the war. I have gained a greater freedom of handling, due largely to the fact that I had to make the rapidest sketches in dangerous positions, and a greater sense of rhythm. I have been jolted.
>
> (Imperial War Museum, 1988)

More recently the curator, Mark Nash, suggested that 'When Langlands and Bell, for example, were commissioned to visit Afghanistan as war artists, the social and political reality they observed transformed their practice, producing an important series of works' (Nash, 2006, p 49).

The suggestion that war acts as a catalyst for 'important' art, complements a common justification of war that it defends and invigorates a vaguely defined set of higher or universal values. In an address to Congress soon after the US and UK invasion of Iraq, Tony Blair claimed, 'Ours are not Western values. They are the universal values of the human spirit' (Blair, 2003).

Terry Eagleton (1990) argues that the very idea of universal values is ideological, because it allows the state to dress up its own interests as being for the ultimate good. The romantic myth of art reinforces this idea by setting up a realm of value apparently above society and politics. And official war art provides a link between this realm of supposedly universal value, and the violent enforcement of partisan interests in war.

This section has identified two ways in which official war art works as propaganda, both centred on the artist in the war zone. Whereas a positivist idea of witness restricts the content of official war art to things seen in the war zone, a romantic idea of art suggests that the extreme experiences encountered there will inspire great art, achieving the 'higher' values invoked by politicians as a justification of war.

For this reason, ideas about witnessing and art became a central part of my attempt to reverse official war art. The project began, however, with the simple intention of drawing the arms trade.

The arms trade

In his farewell address to the US electorate in 1961, President Eisenhower coined the phrase 'military–industrial complex' to describe a network of alliances between arms manufacturers, governments and armed forces which, he warned, exerted a dangerous influence on foreign policy. Since then, the arms industry has grown and expanded. When military budgets fell at the end of the cold war there was a brief opportunity to redirect military production to other purposes. Instead, arms manufacturers merged into vast transnational corporations, and diversified into security. Solomon Hughes (2007) describes this new network as a 'security–industrial complex' and suggests that it influenced the idea of a 'war on terror'. Conjuring up a vague but ever-present threat, the phrase 'war on terror' has been used to justify two wars, increases in military spending and drastic restrictions of civil liberties. In 2003, the year that the US and the UK invaded Iraq, shares in BAE Systems[2] tripled in value (BAE Systems, 2005, p 64).

The influence of the arms trade is not only evident in UK and US foreign policy, but also in the military spending of developing countries. In 1999 BAE Systems sold £2.3 billion worth of Hawk Jets and Gripen Fighters to South Africa. Andrew Feinstein, a former ANC MP, campaigned against the 'inexplicable decision' arguing that it diverted money from health care at a time when South Africa faced an AIDS epidemic but no military threats (Feinstein, 2007, p 232). A BAE contract to supply an Air Defence System to Tanzania in 2001 was equally contentious. Costing £28 million it represented a third of the country's national expenditure on education. In a public statement reminiscent of Feinstein's remarks about the South African deal, the World Bank expressed puzzled concern about the relevance of the equipment to Tanzania. 'We are concerned that such a large expenditure is going to purposes whose justification is not clear to us' (BBC, 2001).

The Serious Fraud Office is currently investigating allegations of bribery in both cases. Such enquiries are politically contentious. In 2006 the British government intervened to prevent a similar investigation of an arms deal between BAE Systems and Saudi Arabia. This history of 'inexplicable' deals, allegations of bribery and stalled prosecutions seems evidence of the network of alliances between arms manufacturers and governments that Eisenhower warned of. However, because this network operates outside official policy, and occasionally outside the law, it is difficult to pin down.

The arms trade is perhaps most visible at arms fairs, vast trade exhibitions where defence and security corporations showcase products to an international clientele. Two of the largest are held in Europe on alternate years – Eurosatory in Paris, and DSEi in London. A smaller arms fair also takes place biennially as part of the Farnborough Air Show. Although DSEi was privatised in 1999 it is given logistical, political and financial support from the UK government. The government invites international delegations, provides security and gives the fair official endorsement through the attendance of ministers. In spite of this, the guest list regularly includes countries that the Foreign and Commonwealth Office considers of 'major concern' in relation to human rights, such as Colombia, China, Iraq, Pakistan, Saudi Arabia and Vietnam (www.caat.org.uk/armsfairs/dsei.php accessed 2 September 2009).

So, if I was going to draw the arms trade, DSEi seemed a good place to start. However, this was easier said than done. The fair is surrounded by the new security that accompanied the 'war on terror'. Since 2001 DSEi has been held at the Excel exhibition centre in Docklands. In her analysis of the creeping privatisation of Britain's urban spaces, Anna Minton (2009) suggests that Excel was designed partly as a fortress. The estates manager claims that, when necessary, the centre can be surrounded by a 'ring of steel' (Minton, 2009, p 13). A towering edifice of iron and concrete, it is geographically isolated from neighbouring communities by the docks on one side, and Docklands Light Railway on the other. The roads into Excel are private, protected by a series of security barriers, and the only other access is by two footbridges from the nearest railway station, Customs House. When Excel hosts controversial events like DSEi or the G20 meeting in 2009, the footbridges are closed to the public and operate as checkpoints. This level of security is maintained through a loose alliance of private security firms, the Ministry of Defence, and the Metropolitan and British Transport police. There was widespread press coverage about the use of anti-terrorism legislation to stop and search protestors at DSEi in 2003. Less publicity was given to the concurrent use of the 1824 Vagrancy Act to prohibit 'loitering' within a kilometre of the fair. This has made it seemingly impossible to get near DSEi whether in curiosity, to protest, or to draw.

Drawing the arms trade

I arrived at Customs House early on the first morning of DSEi 2003, on a train crowded with exhibitors and official guests, each wearing a pass, and protestors.

The police hustled everyone without a pass off the platform and on to a road, separated from Excel by a series of barbed wire fences, railway lines, sidings and a car park. Those who refused to move were carried away. I obediently began to follow police instructions until I noticed that queues of officials were forming at the checkpoints on the footbridges. Realising that this was probably the most I would see of DSEi, I followed the example of the recalcitrant protestors and sat down. I quickly unpacked a sketchbook and ink, and began to draw. But my bravado was short-lived. I was immediately surrounded by security guards and police, and could hardly use my hand for shaking. The fear subsided when I realised the police were arguing about the technicalities of the legislation. One noted that because I was drawing, I couldn't be accused of loitering. And unlike photography, the drawings weren't recognisable so they couldn't be deemed a terrorist threat. Another insisted that drawing people was a breach of their human rights. But, perhaps because the police were photographing me at the time, no one pursued this. So I was left to draw.

At the following DSEi in 2005, only pass holders were allowed off the train at Customs House. So I stayed on and travelled up and down the Docklands line, making rushed drawings of DSEi exhibitors and guests in transit. After a while I noticed I was being followed by a security guard. He hovered half-a-carriage-length away, getting off at the same stations as I did and on to the same trains. Irrationally, I tried to lose him by jumping off at Blackwall just as the train doors closed. This was futile. I was met on the station by a group of transport police. They said that I had been noticed, drawing, and asked to see my credentials. When I explained that I had no credentials, they seemed unsure what to do next. Trains to Blackwall are infrequent mid-morning, so we stood in awkward silence. When the next train arrived they ignored me as I got on, so I resumed drawing.

None of this is unusual. Protestors are regularly stopped, searched, moved on and occasionally arrested for leafleting, walking in groups of more than two, shouting or holding banners in the area around Excel. This perhaps raises the question why they bother to come. Many explain their presence as 'a witness'. Irving Stowe, one of the founders of Greenpeace, defines this sense of witness as 'simply turning up and being at the site of the activity to which they object' (Mulvaney, 1996, p 9).

The idea is that 'simply turning up' is an effective way to protest against a contested activity or event. Deriving from the marginal sense of witness as conviction, this is a very different usage to the eyewitness of official war art. Instead of a noun referring to a detached observer, it is a verb, describing an oppositional presence that deliberately asserts an alternative point of view.

In addition to reversing the focus of official war art, I began to use this oppositional idea of witness as a rationale for drawing the arms trade. But, although the oppositional stance was reflected in the activity of drawing, it wasn't evident in the drawings. When I first drew exhibitors queuing to get in to DSEi, I worked with a mixture of horror and fascination but without a strategy. I assumed that simply by drawing the queue, the politics of the arms trade would somehow be manifest in the drawings. It wasn't. The drawings just depicted men, and occasionally women, in suits. Those that were drawn at an angle as I looked up from the platform even had a heroic quality.

At about this time, a new protest group called CIRCA[3] or the Clandestine Insurgent Rebel Clown Army developed a performance-based, satirical variation of the oppositional witness. In addition to 'turning up' at contested events, CIRCA parody the rituals that define the events. Wearing colanders as helmets, they mimic police uniforms. Carrying papier mache bombs and fake passes, they mock DSEi credentials. Sharing a salute, and combining camouflage with fluorescent pink, they parody army etiquette and dress. Although such rituals may seem trivial, they are key mechanisms through which power is held in place. Outside DSEi a sign warns that visitors must wear business, military or service dress. Here, dress codes bestow status, denote rank and cloak corporate arms dealing in a decorous façade. Because such codes are intended to inspire and denote respect, they are perhaps most effectively undermined by satire. Walter Benjamin noted the power of humour: 'There is no better starting point for thought than laughter; speaking more precisely, spasms of the diaphragm generally offer better chances for thought than spasms of the soul' (1977, p 101).

The CIRCA satirical witness began to influence my method of drawing. Like observational drawing, a CIRCA parody is based on close examination of the subject. In a description of their methods CIRCA stress, 'This requires keen observation and the ability to perceive every detail of a situation' (CIRCA, 2007).

However, in contrast to observational drawing, CIRCA exaggerate and distort the details they perceive. This is closer to caricature. So, following the example of CIRCA, I began to combine observational drawing with caricature.

This method was also influenced by George Grosz's drawings of the Weimar Republic. Grosz was part of Dada, a cultural movement that emerged in reaction to the First World War. Grosz stressed that Dada was not only opposed to the war but to the culture that produced it, particularly the idea that art represented 'higher' values. 'Dada was not a "made" movement, but an organic product, originating in reaction to the head-in-the clouds tendency of so-called holy art, whose disciples brooded over cubes and Gothic art while the generals were painting in blood' (Grosz and Herzfelde, 1925/1992, p 451).

Educated at the Academy of Dresden and the Berlin School of Arts, Grosz learned to draw by copying 'old master' drawings. But when he drew the Weimer Republic, he exchanged the conventions of the academy for those he found on the walls of urinals. 'I copied the folk drawings in urinals, because they seemed to me to convey strong feelings with the greatest economy and immediacy' (Grosz, in Whitford, 1997, p 37).

By using the stylistic conventions of toilet graffiti, Grosz avoided shrouding his subject in the 'higher' values associated with academic drawing.

I tried new venues. I bought a single share in BAE Systems so I could draw inside its annual general meeting. BAE Systems is the world's second largest arms manufacturer, producing fighter jets, war ships, tanks, armoured vehicles, artillery systems, missiles and a range of munitions. An AGM is mainly a PR exercise where accounts from the previous year are presented to shareholders in as favourable a light as possible. However, as unions have begun to lobby pension funds to invest ethically, there is also increasing pressure for companies to appear to be socially responsible. This poses a particular dilemma for BAE Systems which traverses a delicate balance between celebrating the profits that have arisen from wars in Iraq and Afghanistan, while avoiding giving the impression that war is good for business. This contradiction is obfuscated by an aura of civility. The board of directors wear immaculate suits, deferential staff serve lunch with wine, napkins and Mozart, and there is perfume in the toilets. I attempted to undermine the gentility of the event by depicting it in a 'vulgar' way – scribbling the pinstriped suits, floral dresses, piled up pastries and flanks of salmon. Whenever I noticed a gesture or expression that contradicted the polite façade, I exaggerated it. I drew people eating with tongues exposed and crumbs erupting from their mouths, a lecherous advance, a snarl and grimace. To evoke the network of alliances that underpin the arms trade I drew people gossiping, flirting, jostling for position in the pastry queue and knocking back wine. I drew a shareholder so she resembled a vulture, her companion ferreting in a purse, and a company director sniffing his colleague's suit. I learned to draw with one eye on security guards, hiding my notebook when they approached.

But this method raised a new problem. I had caricatured the polite façade that surrounds the arms trade, but the arms trade itself was missing. By scribbling shareholders' outfits, manners and lunch, my criticisms seemed to be directed at people rather than the institutional basis of the arms trade. Offering weapons as commodities, putting exchange value before use, the arms trade cannot be separated from capitalism. However, this economic and political aspect of the arms trade seemed invisible. How could I draw the exchange of weapons as commodities if there were none to be seen? Then, on a whim, I applied for a pass to DSEi as a war artist. That this worked, says a lot about dominant assumptions about war art.

Although I had spent five years drawing outside DSEi, I was totally unprepared for what I found inside. I had become used to reticence about weapons sales. Police announcements describe DSEi as 'a major exhibition'. Dick Olver, the chair of BAE Systems, avoids any reference to arms, talking only of 'security' and 'defence' (Olver, 2007). But there is nothing discreet about DSEi. Tanks, missiles and remote missile launchers dominate two vast halls. There are warships outside in the docks, and fighter jets on the tarmac. Women in low-cut blouses give away sweets in the shape of military trucks, and bouncy balls stencilled with soldier faces. A sales rep hands out toy missiles, and every now and then gives a demonstration by shooting one into the neighbouring display. Video screens show tanks, soldiers and explosions edited, MTV style, to Mariah Carey. Mannequins hang from the ceiling, and guns are lined up like a fairground shooting game. And between the racks of missiles, tables are laid with tablecloths, fruit, canapés and champagne. I began to satirise the marketing strategies of the fair. I drew chemical protection suits lined up like a fashion display at Top Shop, a rep gazing at a mannequin in adoration, a businessman aiming a rifle and another squashing his pinstriped suit into a tank. I drew the free beer and pretzels, olives on cocktail sticks and the sense that it was all just one big party. As in the AGMs, I caricatured alliances between people but here I placed the jokes, back slaps and leers against a backdrop of weapons.

Dissatisfied that the drawings did not adequately convey the incongruity of the slogans, sweeteners and political manipulation, or perhaps because I was becoming affected by the strangeness of the event, I began to exaggerate more wildly. To evoke the sexualising of weapons I added in bras, lace and tongues. I began a conventional drawing of two sales reps in front of a sign promising 'force protection' and then, struck by the ambiguity of the term, drew the male rep's arm stretching aggressively around his reluctant female colleague's shoulders. I drew a saleswoman promoting 'insensitive munitions', and then invented vicious protruding breasts. Some drawings perhaps strayed too far from the actuality of the event. Yet, to draw only from observation would be to take the claims of the arms trade at face value. Occasionally, however, the displays were so bizarre that there was no need to exaggerate. The following year at Eurosatory the Israeli arms manufacturer, Rafael, staged a fashion show as part of a promotion of 'made-to-measure' tank components. As gaunt models swaggered down a catwalk in front of missiles named 'Lethality' and 'Spike', to Handel's 'Queen of Sheba', the only challenge was to depict the spectacle before it passed.

I drew in one more arms fair under the guise of a war artist after that. Then I was found out. While I was drawing in the trade section of the Farnborough air show, a hand fell on my shoulder and a security guard peered into my face. He said had seen me drawing in DSEi, a BAE AGM and now here. Where was my pass? When I showed him, he was momentarily flawed by my status as a war artist. Then he said, 'If you are a war artist, why don't you go and draw in Iraq? Or at least draw things the way they look'. And he asked me to leave.

Afterword

In terms of narrative structure, that should mark the end of my attempt to draw the arms trade. And for a time, I thought it did. My application to DSEi in 2009 was refused. But, in keeping with the oppositional witness, I turned up anyway.

As in previous years, only pass holders were allowed off the train at Customs House. But this time there was a complication. The trains were full of agitated businessmen and women complaining that although their applications had been accepted by email, their passes hadn't arrived. They were instructed to get off at a different stop and take their emails to an improvised security desk where they would be issued with a pass. The queue stretched from the station, across a car park to a marquee. Here, a bus ferried people to loading bays beneath Excel where they queued again. It was unusually hot. Across the tarmac people removed ties, wiped away sweat, abandoned stilettos and swore. Clearly, something had gone wrong with the security. So, although I had no emailed proof of admission, I joined the end of the queue. And when I reached the security desk the staff seemed so weary of complaints that they just let me in.

So, what started as a project to draw the arms trade has become an exercise in stripping away veneers. By reversing the focus, medium and method of official war art, I have attempted to undermine the romantic aura of war art as a source of higher values. By caricaturing the sexualisation of weapons, sweeteners and illicit liaisons of arms fairs, I have tried to subvert the facade of respectability that surrounds arms dealing. And, by using the oppositional idea of witness as a guiding principle, I have managed to get behind a surprisingly fallible wall of security.

Notes

1 Although the term 'war on terror' is now rarely used, the US and UK continue to wage war against an amorphous enemy. In March 2009 the US Defence Department changed the name of the *Global War on Terror* to the *Overseas Contingency Operation* (Wilson and Al Kamen, 2009). Even so, in his Inaugural Address on 20 January 2009, Barack Obama referred obliquely to a 'war against a far-reaching network of violence and hatred' (Obama, 2009).
2 BAE Systems is the world's second largest arms manufacturer. The growth of the company in the first decade of the twenty-first century provides an example of the globalisation of the arms trade. Formed in 1999 from a merger of two UK defence companies, Marconi and British Aerospace, and since acquiring Vickers, a tank manufacturer, BAE describes itself as 'a global defence, security and aerospace company' (www.baesystems.co.uk). Although BAE Systems is often nostalgically described in the UK as a British arms manufacturer it has headquarters in six countries, employs more people in the US than in Britain and supplies military equipment to 100 countries.
3 Formed in 2003 to protest against President Bush's visit to the UK and growing in 2005 during the G8 protests, CIRCA is a network of affinity groups who use clowning and performance as a form of protest.

References

BAE Systems (2005) *Annual Report 2004*, London: BAE Systems..
Barbanell, E. and Garrett, D. (1997) *Encyclopaedia of Empiricism*, London: Fitzroy Dearborn Publishers.
BBC (2001) 'Tanzania "Needs Costly Radar System"', BBC News, 21 December news.bbc.co.uk/1/hi/uk_politics/1723728.stm, accessed 1 September 2009.
Benjamin, Walter (1977) *Understanding Brecht*, London: Stanley Mitchell.
Bush, George W. (2001) *Address to Joint Session of Congress Following 9/11 Attacks*, 20 September www.americanrhetoric.com/speeches/gwbush911jointsessionspeech.htm, accessed 10 October 2009.
Blair, Tony (2003) *Prime Minister's Speech to the United States Congress*, 18 July www.number10.gov.uk/Page4220, accessed 11 February 2010.
CIRCA (2007) *About the Army*, www.clownarmy.org/about/about.html, accessed 10 October 2009.
Cork, Richard (1992) 'Artist defends Mickey Mouse in the Gulf', *The Times*, 15 January.
Craig, Edward (ed.) (1998) *Routledge Encyclopaedia of Philosophy*, London: Routledge.
Daneff, T. and Stringer, R. (1992) 'Mickey Mouse on the Road to Hell', *The London Evening Standard*, 13 January.
Dorman, Arabella (2009) *Front Lines – Images from Iraq*, KBR.
Eagleton, Terry (1990) *The Ideology of the Aesthetic*, Oxford: Blackwell.
Eisenhower, Dwight D. (1961) *Farewell Address*, 17 January www.americanrhetoric.com/speeches/dwightdeisenhowerfarewell.html, accessed 25 July 2009.
Feinstein, Andrew (2007) *After the Party, A Personal and Political Journey inside the ANC*, Jeppestown: Jonathan Ball.

Gillie, Oliver (1992) 'Gulf Artist Defends Scene of War', *The Telegraph*, 16 January.

Gough, Paul (1994) 'The Tyranny of Seeing', *Art Review*, November.

Grosz, George and Herzfelde, Wieland (1925) 'Art is in Danger' in Harrison, C. and Wood, P. (eds) (1992) *Art in Theory 1900–1990*, Oxford: Blackwell.

Harris, Jonathan (2006) *Art History, The Key Concepts*, Abingdon: Routledge.

Hughes, Solomon (2007) *War on Terror, inc.* London and New York: Verso.

Imperial War Museum (1982) *Linda Kitson Press Cuttings*, Department of Art: Unpublished Collection of Press Cuttings.

Imperial War Museum (1988) *Paul Nash, Through the Fire: Paintings, Drawings and Graphic Work from the First World War*, London: Imperial War Museum.

Lewise R.E. (ed.) (2000) *Middle English Dictionary*, University of Michigan Press.

Malvern, Susan (2004) *Modern Art, Britain and the Great War: Witnessing, Testimony and Remembrance*, New Haven and London: Yale University Press.

Minton, Anna (2009) *Ground Control*, London: Penguin.

Mulvaney, Kieran (1996) *Witness: Greenpeace – 25 Years on the Environmental Front Line*, André Deutsch.

Nash, Paul (1949) *Outline: An Autobiography*, London: Faber and Faber.

Nevinson, C.R.W., Lavery, J., Nash, P. and Kennington, E. (1918) *British Artists at the Front*, London: Country Life.

Obama, Barack (2009) *Inaugural Address*, 20 January, www.whitehouse.gov/blog/inaugural-address, accessed 10 October 2009.

Olver, Dick (2007) *Opening Address BAE Annual General Meeting*, 9 May.

Searle, Adrian (2007) 'Last Post', *The Guardian*, 12 March www.guardian.co.uk/politics/2007/mar/12/iraq.art accessed 7 October 2009.

Stallabrass, Julian (2004) 'Painting Desert Storm', Review of the John Keane exhibition at the Imperial War Museum, *New Left Review*, no 195, September–October, pp. 102–9.

Tate Britain (2004) *Turner Prize 2004*, London: Tate Publishing.

Thurlbeck Neville (1992) 'War is … Mickey Mouse on a Toilet', *Today*, 14 January.

Whitford, Frank (1997) *The Berlin of George Grosz*, New Haven and London: Yale University Press.

Williams, Raymond (1976) *Keywords*, London: Fontana.

Wilson, Scott and Al Kamen (2009) '"Global War on Terror", is Given New Name', *The Washington Post*, 25 March www.washingtonpost.com/wp-dyn/content/article/2009/03/24/AR2009032402818.html accessed 10 October 2009.

9 Pathways to experiencing war

Christine Sylvester

This collection explores ways to conceptualize war as practices of international collective violence that involve bodily experiences of many kinds. Those experiences run the gamut from physical pain to gender exhilaration, from weighty debates about the human to national and family war memories that haunt today's social relations. There is no punch line at the end of this exercise, no definition, theory, approach, methodology, or set agenda that links and harnesses the insights offered here into "a" research program. Rather, drawing on perspectives from law, history, anthropology, ethics and philosophy, development studies, international relations, and art practice, the collection provides contexts of war and experience in which bodily experiences foreground both the personal and the political. In this concluding chapter, I mark out a few research pathways to consider taking next, hoping that others will come along on these journeys or create pathways of their own to understanding and theorizing war as experience.

What is war today?

There is a sense running through this collection that the oft-asked question of war in our time – what is it? – is not (yet?) resolvable when aspects of experience are considered along with military-like actions on a large scale. There are numerous types of actors, activities, goals, strategies, weapons, ethics, gender considerations, and historical contexts to consider. War, living beings, experience, and politics – it is quite a messy equation to think of simplifying, deconstructing, or even quantifying. Perhaps, therefore, it makes sense to focus on realms or locations of important knowledge about war that the contributors identify. Clearly there is a legal/ethical/organizational realm, and it includes international law, issues of moral authority, United Nations resolutions, and gender ethics. Anne Orford, Kimberly Hutchings, Brigitte Holzner, and Megan MacKenzie sort through those issues here, particularly as they relate to a trendsetting type of war in our time: humanitarian intervention. Another realm of war today highlights shifting locations of war making and technological/strategic changes that affect how war is conducted and experienced. This set of issues emerges in Stephen Chan's and Jill Gibbon's contributions. A third way into the war question focuses on ordinary people's experiences of war as they relate them, compared to the ways academics, the state, and media evaluate experiences conveyed secondhand; the chapters by MacKenzie and Kwon are especially pertinent to such issues. One might think of these three realms as incipient research tracks that could be incorporated into a larger research agenda on experiencing war.

Legal/ethical/organizational challenges

Is war a form of humanitarianism in our time? One would think so given the way that humanitarian intervention has been hailed in some international law and organization settings. It is the use of state-orchestrated military violence to stop "rogue," "evil," or vengeance-wreaking states from killing groups in the very populations a sovereign state is supposed to protect from outside harm. A new respectability has been accorded the use of force as a response to humanitarian challenges (as in Bosnia) and as a means of closing down and clearing out regimes that the West finds threatening or recalcitrant (e.g. Saddam Hussein's Iraq). Under the UN charter, member states can use collective security to deter illegal uses of violence. But is it humanitarian to halt unwarranted state violence through externally imposed military violence? Or is there a relationship between ends and means that cannot be ignored, a relationship which always already privileges war over the saving of lives?

Orford notes in one of her earlier works that the human rights legal community has generally applauded the new acceptance of forceful intervention as a system norm. They have seen humanitarian intervention as one key way to drive home the point that a diverse citizenry is legitimate in today's nations and no state-determined standard of ethnicity, religion, gender, or age can be conjured as a way of stripping groups of citizens of rights and, most importantly, of their lives. But what a contradictory approach this is to upholding human rights! It requires determining how much suffering is enough to warrant legal violent intervention relative to suffering that does not quite make the interventionist grade. How many deaths are required before international law courts, or the Security Council of the UN, can decide that force is a warranted form of intervention by the international community and not tantamount to an illegal invasion of a sovereign state? Hutchings asks similar questions about moral authority for a humanitarianism expressed through war. Universal human rights are often mentioned as a reason why an interventionist move is required, but Hutchings wonders whether, in practice, there is any stable sense of the human as reference point in rights practice. Is not the human always gendered in theory and in fact? And does not gender enter into judgments about the kind of suffering that merits intervention, which humans are suffering and need rescuing, which humans can be killed in order to be kind to those identified as the suffering humans, and who has the responsibility and capability to intervene? The calibration problematic that Orford raises with respect to international law courts – how much of this and that horror can justify intervention? – applies to issues of moral judgment and authority, too. So also do forms of judgment that slice the human up into power capabilities and award (or punish) the most capable with the responsibility to determine who to help in which ways.

Philosophical questions like those raised by Orford and Hutchings bounce back and forth in multiple arcs of debate today. It is therefore of some interest that Orford ends her discussion by directing attention away from the questions she poses starkly to an action that encapsulates them. A tapestry copy of Pablo Picasso's *Guernica* is covered over with a blue cloth, and is further obscured with flags in front, when then Secretary of State Colin Powell arrives in 2003 to address the Security Council. Powell wants to persuade that body to intervene militarily in Iraq so as to preempt the use of its weapons of mass destruction against others. Orford interprets the cover-up as a politics of avoidance – avoiding a visual display of sovereign state authority to kill on the eve of a negotiation about who may kill whom for what humanitarian reasons. Franco's attack on the town of Guernica in the 1930s, universally considered an unmitigated atrocity, is not something the UN apparently wants viewers to connect in any way to the war discussion unfolding in the world's major peace organization. Why? Because the scene shows terrified women and children and bellowing animals experiencing aerial bombardment. That moment captured by Picasso's famous painting and copied on the tapestry is soul-wrenching, not for the reason that the cause behind the attack was as unjust as it was, but mainly because the attack terrified people who experienced it, no matter what the rationale for it or who carried it out. So at the moment the most power-capable state in the state system is about to present its case for humanitarianism as war, the organization of sovereign states decides that acknowledging experiences of war on the ground is best camouflaged.

What is war when it is said to be humanitarian? In effect, it is self- or allied- or UN-authorized use of violence against bodies on the ground. The intriguing agenda-setting question that Orford raises is whether it is appropriate to trust decision making on such a timely but convoluted type of warring to international organizations and law courts. Are not the issues so philosophically weighty that courts must refuse the calibrations asked of them? Yet if courts back away from judgments, then humanitarian intervention can be decided by powerful states alone using advanced military technologies that injure whichever bodies are in the way of the rescue objective. The illusions of humanitarian intervention are multiple, complex, and need continued analysis and critique in any project that puts the emphasis on experience rather than on rights and might.

Gender challenges

Is gender central to the definition of any war? Many Western feminists would argue that it is, pinpointing aspects of masculinity as key elements affecting the persistence and longevity of war as a social institution. In other words, war is largely instigated and sustained by a hyper-masculine politics of force, a politics largely associated with militarized men. Women who buy into that politics and seek power through war and violence are inside the masculinity framework of analysis and therefore are seen as part of a war problematic. Those who oppose war are outside the box, except for the sense that everyone reading this book is militarized and incapable of extricating themselves from the overwhelming influence of war as a global norm and practice. Yet several contributors to this volume cast some doubt on this established feminist formulation. They do so not because they themselves fail to sympathize with the argument, but because they study women who have far more complicated experiences with war than much feminist scholarship has theorized to date.

Until recently, gender arenas of power relations were missing from most studies of contemporary war, whether conducted by conventional war studies researchers or by feminists. War was defined, implicitly rather than explicitly, as organized collective violence conducted in the main by men, leaving women as hapless victims affected by, but themselves outside, the politics of war making. That gender is less neglected today with respect to war and not just peace topics is testament to gender scholars in academia and in national and international organizations. Brigitte Holzner has been in all three locations and has seen war across the world. Her contribution to this volume genders specific types of war worries that Orford and Hutchings study in more general terms. Holzner presents UN peacekeepers as whiling away time near the town of Srebrenica drawing offensive pictures of Bosnian women on their barrack walls. When a gender massacre occurs outside those barracks – with Bosnian men killed and the women shipped out – the official humanitarians freeze. They either decide to do nothing to stop the killing or are emotionally and physically unable to act amidst a war frenzy that can suddenly turn on them. That tragic stumble in peacekeeping logic and practice sets in motion a debate about associating peacekeeping as a UN activity and peacekeeper men (mainly) with protective activities in war zones. Another way of saying this is that war once again trumps humanitarianism in certain humanitarian interventionist situations.

In the Liberian civil wars, gender enters the picture very visibly and cannot be missed as an ingredient in war and in peace. In that conflict zone, women become active in the war using at least two noteworthy political capacities. Some among them, who have already been kidnapped by militias and subjected to physical assault, join the war fighting. They do so, however, on their own terms and those terms suggest that they reconfigure the conflagration as a gender war of revenge against women-hurting compatriots. Gun-toting killers of considerable notoriety and skill, organized and led by the woman warrior Black Diamond, outdo many of the men around them in war ferocity and courage. The feminist irony in their situation is that the women are not masculinized exactly, because although their bravado stems from militarization, it is directed against macho militarized men. Perhaps this is their version of humanitarian intervention: kill men to be kind to women. The more famous group of women for peace is even more effective than its killer counterparts. These women eventually persuade the embattled head of state, Charles Taylor, to attend peace talks in Ghana and then determinedly occupy the building until a peace agreement is reached. The women killers and those insistent on peace are both home-grown Liberians. They have differing experiences of class, age, and social respect anchoring their respective politics, but in both cases, women take some command in the local politics of warring. Those intriguing facts cannot be overlooked in theorizing war as experience. It is important to note the spectacle of an international community stewing over which type of suffering deserves an interventionist response, while effective forms of politics, deadly and peaceful, emerge locally and operate mostly without outside help. All the huffing and puffing in the Security Council, all the scrambling of fighter planes to humanitarian crises in other places can be very much beside the point for women living with war outside humanitarian-assisted conflict zones.

Switch to women as soldiers in Sierra Leone. The stories they tell Megan MacKenzie about their war experiences contrast sharply with the analyses of war that shape the work of international organizations. Holzner finds that the UN admirably engages women's involvement in war and post-conflict politics and crystallizes gender concerns within a number of resolutions. UNSCR 1325 requires, among other things, that women and women's concerns appear in peace and conflict resolution operations, while UNSCR 1820 condemns sexual violence in war. Even so, these resolutions assume that wartime atrocities are instigated and carried out by men, thus reinforcing old stereotypes of women as far less violent than men, inside or outside situations of armed conflict. MacKenzie's work in tandem with Holzner's conclusions shows that women's many activities in war are still not being taken seriously enough by institutions that have resources to assist them. Some contemporary philosophy of sovereignty and exception can also marginalize women, which does not help anyone get out from under gendered constraints and circumscribed roles. Return to Hutching's point about the dangers of believing that a universal human exists as an ungendered basis of humanitarianism today, or that it is possible to rewrite war from feminist perspectives without tackling the fictions that determine which gendered bodies are likely to be on the receiving end of bombardments in the name of humanitarianism or justice. Unreal stick figures haunt the lore of war to such a degree that variegated women of war can get only incomplete and idealized attention by international bodies like the UN. Defining war in experiential terms requires considerably more research on the gender ghosts rattling around dominant war narratives in international law and international organizations.

War's old venues and techniques

Heonik Kwon takes the reader to a particular type of war associated with a short but profound period of international relations: the cold war, circa 1945 to 1989/91. That moment in international relations is usually bracketed on one side by the lingering endgames of World War II, a massive war that seems remarkably old-fashioned in light of humanitarian or terror wars of our time. On the other side of the cold war is the collapsed Berlin Wall and subsequent break-up of the Soviet bloc. Kwon maintains that the cold war, along with its moral parameters, venues, and techniques, is not a settled matter temporally if one focuses on the experiences of people with the hot wars of that era. Most scholarship iterates the sense that the cold war was about ideologies, blocs, and states and not about ordinary people affected by abstract bipolar hostilities. But there were ghastly and lengthy wars in Asia, Africa, and Latin America, which means that many people's lives are full of war experiences, directly and as memories. These lives must be pushed to the top of a cold war research agenda that is still preoccupied with the machinations of power blocs and with the experiences of Western servicemen and women in the wars of the era.

Kwon moves about geospatially while simultaneously creating resemblances of experience across the cold war zones. I admire his ability to connect human experiences of that era from Greece to Korea, Vietnam, and Indonesia without getting bogged down in the details of the wars themselves. His focus is on family issues, confrontations, and silences that emerge around memories of those wars and the people who participated on various sides and possibly lost their lives. People living now might not have experienced the wars themselves; but periodi-cally they face family issues around the dead ancestors who did or the brothers who fought on opposing sides. Kwon tells of small everyday efforts to bridge simmering hurts and thereby bring the dead back home to traumatized families in peace and comradeship. These ghosts of war share the type of fate that some women warriors experience, whose deeds are either not recorded as part of the politics of war in their societies or not spoken of in family settings. Kwon is very comfortable with ghosts and knows how they affect social and political life long after their bodily demise.[1] He knows that the cold war touched the lives of many and that experiences of that time are still being unearthed and played out now. For many, many people, war was so hot during the cold war that it stuck to their flesh.

Like Orford, Kwon also closes his chapter with references to art, a move that reinforces the sense that there is only so much to learn from one discipline or even by going interdisciplinary with cognate subjects. To jog the mind into a different quadrant of knowing and understanding, it can be crucial to engage other forms of sensory acuity, such as art and fictional accounts of war. Kwon refers to the Cubist tradition in which the prized Renaissance technique of giving a flat canvas depth and perspective is refused and flatness is allowed to rein. The result is a background and foreground that converge in space and become equally important to the overall picture. The lesson in that is quite simple but hardly simplistic: put the people usually assigned the background in cold war studies right up alongside the usually starring superpowers in the true north of cold war international rela-tions. Then see what the cold war looks like.

Visual art is precisely what Jill Gibbon does all the time. In this volume, she crosses over from the world of art drawing to the land of academic war studies, carrying her pictures with her. And she does so while telling the reader of the experiences she has had while endeavoring to capture hidden or unnoted aspects of contemporary war without relying on words as points of entry. Art making and art experience can reveal and articulate puzzles that lie beyond the boundaries of art practice. And, art practices can also inspire research methodologies that depart considerably from both art-making techniques and from social science, law, his-tory, and other disciplinary patterns.[2] Gibbon draws the arms trade, itself a wild idea when juxtaposed with social science ways of thinking about arms and about global trade. To do her research, she must get into arms fairs in the UK without an invitation, and then draw quickly and inconspicuously so as not to get evicted from the premises. Once in, Gibbon interprets and brings to light ghostly ambiguities that lurk behind the politics of humanitarian war deliberations at the United Nations and other venues. To do so requires acts of art and of political defiance in spaces between war protester and war artist.

What a way to do research! Those who never think of drawing international relations, yet alone a puzzle as difficult to picture precisely as the arms trade, get a lesson from Gibbon in new activities, challenges, and approaches to fieldwork. Gibbon was not in a war zone as such, and yet she was. Personally opposed to war and not keen on war art as propaganda or the notion that war can unleash great artistic achievement, she becomes witness, observer, spy, and interpreter of a politics that is off radar. She simultaneously chronicles the existence and modus operandi of the fairs, deconstructs social interactions among arms traders and clients, and caricatures the ambiance of weapons as sexy and trade fairs as fashionable. Hers is a methodology within a methodology: at once she is a researcher trying to get "data" in a place that does not welcome researchers, and she is recording her data visually and interpretively. The resulting work offers a serious critique of the military–industrial complex as it shows itself off today, with its complex "fair" security systems and its miniaturized weapons given as toys or souvenirs. There is a gain in visual acuity in her exercise and lessons on how to do politics while also doing research on war.

Stephen Chan is another contributor who gets into the fray of international politics, frequently, and all around Africa. Here, Chan draws word pictures of contemporary wars in Africa and critiques their casting as "new wars." It is said that the advent of humanitarian interventionist war is the consequence of changing warfare in a post-cold-war time and space that is not segmented and policed with the obsessiveness of bipolarity. Today's wars can often be traced back to cold war politics, as Kwon points out, but they exceed the wars of that time in brutality, meaninglessness, and in the degree of local state failure to govern on any level. Chan's main critique of new war thinking is that what seems new is only so if one has a short memory of war. "New" wars can seek old goals – control of a state – and are just as barbarous as the Dresden fire bombing, Auschwitz, atomic bombs over Japan, or massacred villagers in My Lai, Vietnam. Moreover, all these new and old wars are modern wars using modern technologies. Chan's discussion of the battles to secure Uganda presses these points and adds to them the modern state strategy of leveraging off one's enemies instead of ending their attacks. He also argues that each post-cold-war conflict has particular sources, manifestations, and supports: Bosnia is not Liberia is not Sudan, which means that a blanket term like "new wars" might be inappropriate. Although there is little we have not seen before in all these wars, Chan argues that there is something that would be new if it were taken up systematically in research, namely, efforts to engage empathetically with people who are used, sliced into pieces, and then ignored in the wars of our time. What would their war experiences suggest about ways to differentiate wars, based on how they are experienced rather than how they are fought? To ask those questions is to treat war in a new way rather than proclaim that the goals, methods, and practices of wars today are new.

So, what is war? It is much the old story of large-scale collective violence; but it works with myriad more actors, all of whom experience the collective violence differently depending on their location, level and mode of involvement, gender, moral code, memories, and access to technologies. The issue, we learn, is not getting the fine points of a definition right – Chan's argument strongly suggests that exercises like that are bound to fail. At issue is getting the experiences of collective violence recorded and analyzed as part of international relations and war studies. The contributors to this volume join others in hoisting such a focus off the ground. Yet we must remember the ghosts about. The task of shifting to war as experience rather than remaining with war as strategy *et al.* requires that the researcher research differently by operating on the elusive terrain of emotional as well as physical experiences with war.

War as experience and politics

Does what one does relate to what one feels and thinks? Are the things we feel and think socialized to be at the service of masters other than ourselves? Are people trapped in someone else's material or ideological narrative of life or war? Are they so hammered down by the habits and patterns of daily living that the senses are jaded, or so numbed that experiences pass unnoticed? Do you need experience to have experiences? Can everyone claim unique or personally nuanced experiences, or are war experiences like weapons that can be counted, tallied up, summarized? Again, there will be multiple answers to these questions and many ways of framing the questions themselves. Rather than settle the matter of what experience is before actually doing the research, it might make sense to derive war experiences from the ways people describe them – in art, in novels and testimonials, in and out of uniform, and with bomb strapped to waist or baby on the back.

Exploring emotional dissonances and displays

One way into the labyrinth of war experience is through a methodology that can be tested on us as researchers in the first instance, in order to discover our own physical, emotional, and intellectual tasks, reactions, and feelings about war. That methodology entails identifying, thinking about, and working with emotional dissonances that can crop up in researchers' lives when war or certain wars are described in ways that seem to leave something out. A moment in Rey Chow's *The Age of the World Target* provides a sense of what emotional dissonance feels like and can lead to. Growing up among survivors of the Japanese invasion of China in 1937 and occupation of the country until 1945, she writes,

> As a child, I was far more accustomed to hearing about Japanese atrocities against Chinese men and women during the war than I was to hearing about U.S. atrocities against Japan. Among the stories of the war was how the arrival of the Americans brought relief, peace, and victory for China; however hard the times were, it was said to be a moment of "liberation."

As I grow older, this kind of knowledge gathered from oral narratives persists in my mind not as proof of historical accuracy but rather as a kind of emotional dissonance, a sense of something out-of-joint that becomes noticeable because it falls outside the articulations generated by the overpowering image of the mushroom cloud.[3]

Emotions relate to, give expression to, and produce bodily sensations. They also heighten or can be created by what people see, hear, touch, smell, and even taste (imagine how difficult it must be for some people to stop tasting 9/11 soot). Emotions attach to mental activities like memory and emotions can create and sustain new memories, as in the oft-heard remark in the USA, "I'll never forget what I was doing when those planes hit the twin towers." Emotions can also impel people to action, for good or ill, or seize them up so they cannot act, cannot remember, cannot feel; and yet not feeling is an experience as much as is running frantically for cover. What Chow is referring to is a situation of incongruence and incommensurability between the praiseworthy behavior of American military soldiers in putting an end to the Japanese occupation of China, and their appalling behavior in aiming two atom bombs at the Japanese. Her sense of dissonance is the clue to an unresolved and ambiguous circumstance of experience.

Globalization makes it relatively easy for personal–political and cultural emotions to reach wide audiences. The media is always already snapping a photograph and sticking a microphone in a face before moving on to the next hot spot down the line. The mobile phone rings with information. The screen lights up tweets. In war zones, those media messages can be invaluable to all sides in a conflict, including average people seeking to know where the latest fighting is in a miasma of violence. Chan points out that standard studies of new wars raise questions about new causes, new methods, new types of participants, and new irrationalities involved in contemporary conflicts. How the everyday victim of war understands what is happening is not part of the new wars mission.[4] Perhaps that "victim," however, is only part victim, being also part something else, such as suicide bomber, war enthusiast, or loyal wife of the commander. A fourteen-year-old girl is raped in Iraq by US military personnel. That is stark victimhood, no doubt, as are military actions that rely on child soldiers or that feature rape and abuse/torture of men and women. But just as humanitarian intervention kills to be kind, much that happens in a war is not easy to tag ethically. Everyday occurrences take place in grey areas that give rise to emotional dissonances.

One might raise the stakes a bit more, however, by asking whether students of war as experience have the tools to get at these complexities. If a person's face seems to register no emotion, does that indicate indifference, fright, grief, numbness, depression, even joy? Or does it signal ambivalence? It depends on the context. Judith Butler encourages an anti-war politics based on the mutuality of grieving and mourning experienced on all sides in any war. Rey Chow's discussions of her own ambivalent reactions to dominant stories of Chinese liberation by the USA suggest that emotions might not be easy for war subjects, let alone researchers of emotion, to identify. Jean Elshtain said that "wars destroy and bring into being men and women as particular identities by canalizing energy and giving permission to narrate."[5] What if narration comes hard? What if one is changing emotions as one narrates war emotions? Mixed emotions might also be kept hidden as a personal security strategy, a way of fitting in, or to send the researcher on his or her way. To complicate matters more, Erin Manning argues that "sense does not pre-exist experience," suggesting obliquely that experiences with/in war and violence might curdle our senses and render our emotions unreliable as empirical sensors.[6] Accordingly, questions of how to research emotions effectively and ethically must be high on any agenda for theorizing war as experience.

War and daily lived experience

War is such a transhistorical and transcultural phenomenon that it is part of global daily life. It is not that we are all at war but we are all affected by a system milieu in which war continues to feature as a politics of extreme disagreement. Politics might be taking other forms where we live – the ballot box, the letter to one's representative, the local initiative to build a school, the summit of the UN Security Council, a protest march. On any day anywhere in the world, though, there are local and international experiences of war to ponder. Reconfiguring war as experience requires an intellectual–emotional leap towards appreciating that war is commonplace in many people's lives as well as exceptional. It is about the ordinary as well as the extraordinary, the lived experiences of wars that drag on and on, as so many do today. A few final suggestions to consider.

Carry on studying women who war as well as those who refuse to war or are victimized by someone else's war. The woman warrior's experiences are just as valid as the experiences of peace women; and yet warrior women tend to receive less personal and focused research. Perhaps it is easier to locate and study groups of people advocating for a certain social value compared to individuals who go about warring, say, without politicizing their personal or personalizing their political environs of violence. In some circles, such as much Western feminism, to pursue groups and individuals that work for peace and not war would be the correct order of priorities in research and in practice. It makes some sense. Our time seems so consumed with rage and violence that peace appears to be less emphasized than war; even though there are fewer wars today than in the past, peace seems out of fashion. At the same time, to understand war as experience, it does not make sense to decide in advance which and whose experiences are going to be included in the problematic and which ones will be excluded or shoved to the side. To study women of war is not to advocate war or to endorse any particular war. It is simply an act of research inclusiveness that releases an unsettling partial truth into the ether: women war too, and they seem to do so for many reasons still to be explored.

Similarly, it behooves the war-as-experience researcher to spend some time studying war enthusiasts and war's enthusiasms among military, paramilitary, Sunday warriors, and media figures who gravitate toward war zones. Some of those enthusiasts might be one's neighbors. When I lived in the Gettysburg Pennsylvania area years ago, I was always astounded and puzzled by the large numbers of people who arrived every July to re-enact the Gettysburg battle – to "do it ourselves," as one participant once told me. Clearly a re-enactment is theater in a finely mead-owed old place of war. Yet why go through it all in excruciating detail once again? Surely it is not just about re-living history or keeping stories alive. Surely there are other personal and group agendas and dynamics activated by the performance of war enthusiasms. What of those who put themselves in real battle zones time and again and become agitated when they are out of action? Don McCullen, for one, calls his return to civilian ways after a lifetime of war photojournalism a "shocking liberty." It took him away from the latest fray and it took the Thatcher-years print media in the UK away from showing photographs of war to instead showing pho-tographs of fashion models, uptown cars, and bankers entertaining at their Devon country houses. War was and often still is regularly cancelled as news to make room for consumerist or celebrity-stocked experiences of faux struggle. It can be trendy in some quarters to applaud the absence of war images in the press (despite being sent over to commercial film) on the grounds that looking at suffering and violence is the mark of a war tourist, a gawker, a rubbernecker pleased to be safe and merely looking on. As with most such political formulations, the insight that one could help and not look away mingles with self-referential reasons for banish-ing war and its wounds from vision. Yet any war escape today will be only partial. The safe are securitized these days to the point where more and more aspects of life come under surveillance, ostensibly to save citizens from those who would war against this or that land. For all that surveillance, how much visual acuity is achieved? Inescapable wars of our time end up as ghosts themselves, periodically thrust into minute media stories of a suicide bombing or a misdirected missile.

   The texture of war, the experience of war, is both common and unique and it is little wonder that some are put off by it and others are alienated from peace. Several contributors to this volume find textures of war in the arts; but novels have not been mentioned. What lies at the breach point in a fact/fiction line of demarcation? Make believe? Imagination? Creativity? Texture. For me, novels are important points of entry to war as experience. My personal–political does include an experience with war up close. I was at Joshua Nkomo's Bulawayo house at the exact moment Robert Mugabe's troops arrived in 1983 to begin their deadly purge of dissidents from the newly independent country. Nkomo was Mugabe's rival. The Ndebele people resisted Mugabe's charms, although they did so by then mostly at the ballot box and with the emotional dissonance that comes from recognizing the recent liberation from Rhodesian government as good despite the fact that credit was largely withheld from the anti-colonial guerrilla army that Nkomo had commanded. That day in 1983, rifles took aim. Jeeps of grim-looking soldiers surrounded Nkomo's house. Sjamboks were hitting heads and backs outside that house and all along the route from Nkomo's township to the white city center. All of it filled my mind and engaged every sense in ways I had not imagined possible; those images of war refuse erasure.[7] Nonetheless, or rather perhaps because of that personal experience, a well-crafted fictional account of war can impact my research sensibilities like nothing else.

The character called Methode in Gil Courtemanche's novel *A Sunday at the Pool in Kigali*[8] is a stand-out, and I have had occasion to analyze his situation several times.[9] Methode is an AIDS victim and he is a Tutsi in 1994 Rwanda as the Hutu killers take to the streets after people like him. Damned to a miserable death either way, Methode responds by rewriting the choices surrounding his imminent death. As the end looms closer and the Hutu cry of killing the cockroaches roars around him, Methode summons his friends and puts on a performance of pleasure. He has sex with a friend, sex being known as one of Methode's greatest bodily joys. He overdoses on morphine administered by a Canadian development worker, drains a bottle of whiskey, and has a friend film his parting soliloquy. And then he dies. Methode's script of passing stars his body as the ultimate center of experience, in daily life, in war and even in dying. After his spectacular production, he succumbs to AIDS, yes; but he is thrilled that he is not going to die at the hands of genocidal neighbors. In effect, Methode molds the stark options open to him and comes out with something different. The trade-offs involved – AIDS or the chop of a machete – are far from acceptable. Yet the decision Methode makes raises the startling suggestion that in some war circumstances, it can be preferable to die from a disease the UN seeks to eradicate than die at the hands of one's state and citizens. That is the kind of lesson that a novel can highlight or an artist might be able to draw interpretively.

In lieu of a conclusion, let me reiterate the obvious and the less obvious. War experiences come in prosaic, profound, sickening, excruciating, and exhilarating ways, to all kinds of people living inside and outside actual war zones. Experiences of war provide information about what it is, how it operates, who takes part, how they are affected and affecting, and what the politics of war looks like beyond the war rooms of state. To access those experiences takes more than good intentions and interest. It requires that a researcher take a close look at herself/himself and a creative and acute look around at the mundanities and spectaculars, the tears and politics of life that accompany and that shape war. That is the message of *Experiencing War* and its point of departure for theorizing war anew.

Notes

1 Heonik Kwon, *Ghosts of War in Vietnam* (Cambridge: Cambridge University Press, 2008).
2 I develop and illustrate this argument in *Art/Museums: International Relations Where We Least Expect It* (Boulder: Paradigm Publishers, 2009).
3 Rey Chow, *The Age of the World Target: Self-Referentiality in War, Theory, and Comparative Work* (Durham: Duke University Press, 2006), p. 26.
4 This point was discussed at length in two Touching War sessions: on new wars, with Stephen Chan and Jude Murison; and on women and armed conflict with Megan MacKenzie, Christine Masters, Swati Parashar, Corinna Peniston-Bird, Elina Penttinen, and Laura Sjoberg.
5 Jean Bethke Elshtain, *Women and War* (Basic Books, 1987), p. 166.
6 Erin Manning, *Politics of Touch: Sense, Movement, Sovereignty* (Minneapolis: University of Minnesota Press, 2007), p. 131.
7 Christine Sylvester, "An African Dilemma," *The Progressive*, January 1983, pp. 40–43.

8 Gil Courtemanche, *A Sunday at the Pool in Kigali* (London: Canongate, 2003).
9 Christine Sylvester, "Development and Postcolonial Takes on Biopolitics and Economy," in Jane Pollard, Cheryl McEwan, and Alex Hughes (eds) *Postcolonial Economies: Rethinking Material Lives* (Zed, 2011); and "Bare Life as a Development/ Postcolonial Problematic," *Geographical Journal*, 172, 1–2, 2006, pp. 66–77.

Index